SOCIALISM AND LABOR

SOCIALISM AND LABOR

AND OTHER ARGUMENTS

SOCIAL, POLITICAL, AND PATRIOTIC

BY

RT. REV. J. L. SPALDING

𝔅𝔦𝔰𝔥𝔬𝔭 𝔬𝔣 𝔓𝔢𝔬𝔯𝔦𝔞

Essay Index Reprint Series

BOOKS FOR LIBRARIES PRESS, INC.
Freeport, New York

First published 1902
Reprinted 1967

LIBRARY OF CONGRESS CATALOG CARD NUMBER:
67-28768

PRINTED IN THE UNITED STATES OF AMERICA

CONTENTS

SOCIALISM AND LABOR

AND OTHER ARGUMENTS.

I.

SOCIALISM AND LABOR.

THE interest which all who think take in the laboring classes, whether it spring from sympathy or fear, is a characteristic feature of the age.

Their condition seems to be the great anomaly in our otherwise progressive and brilliant civilization. Whether when compared with the lot of the slaves and serfs of former times that of the modern laborer is fortunate, is not the question. He is not placed in the midst of the poverty and wretchedness of a rude and barbarous society, but in the midst of boundless wealth and great refinement. He lives, too, in a democratic age, in which all men profess to believe in equality and liberty; in an age in which the brotherhood of the race is proclaimed by all the organs of opinion. He has a voice in public affairs, and since laborers are the majority, he is, in theory at least, the sovereign.

They who govern profess to do everything by the authority of the people, in their name and for their welfare; and yet, if we are to accept the opinions of the Socialists, the wage-takers, who in the modern world are the vast multitude, are practically shut out from participation in our intellectual and material inheritance. They contend that the poor are, under the present economic system, the victims of the rich, just as in the ancient societies the weak were the victims of the strong; so that wage-labor, as actually constituted, differs in form rather than in its essential results from the labor of slaves and serfs. And even dispassionate observers think that the tendency of the present system is to intensify rather than to diminish the evils which do exist; and that we are moving towards a state of things in which the few will own everything, and the many be hardly more than their hired servants. In America, they admit that sparse population and vast natural resources that as yet have hardly been touched helped to conceal this fatal tendency, which is best seen in the manufacturing and commercial centres of Europe, where the capitalistic method of production has reduced wage-earners to a condition of pauperism and degradation which is the scandal of Christendom and a menace to society.

The present condition of labor is the result of gradually evolved processes, running through centuries.

The failure of the attempt of Charlemagne to organize the barbarous hordes which had overspread Europe into a stable empire was followed by an era of violence and lawlessness, of wars and invasions, from which society sought refuge in the feudal system. The strong man, as temporal or spiritual lord, was at the top of the feudal hierarchy, and under him the weak formed themselves into classes. The serf labored a certain number of days for himself, and a certain number for his lord. In the towns the craftsmen were organized into guilds which protected the interests of the members. The mendicant poor were not numerous, and their wants were provided for by the bishops and the religious orders.

Then the growth of towns and the development of trade and commerce brought wealth to the burghers, who became a distinct class, while domestic feuds and foreign wars, especially the Crusades, weakened and impoverished the knights and barons. The printing-press and the use of gunpowder in war helped further to undermine the feudal power, while the discovery of America, the turning of the Cape of Good Hope, and the Protestant revolution threw all

Europe into a ferment from which new social conditions were evolved. The peasants who had been driven from the land by the decay of the great baronial houses, and the confiscation of the property of the church, flocked into the towns or became vagabonds. The poor became so numerous that permanent provision had to be made for them, and poor laws were consequently devised. It was the contemplation of their misery which caused Sir Thomas More to write the following words, which sound as though they had been taken from some modern Socialist address:

" Therefore, I must say that, as I hope for mercy, I can have no notion of all the other governments that I see or know than that they are a conspiracy of the rich, who on pretence of managing the public, only pursue their private ends, and devise all the ways and arts they can find out; first that they may without danger preserve all that they have so ill acquired, and then that they may engage the poor to toil and labor for them at as low rates as possible, and oppress them as much as they please. And if they can but prevail to get these contrivances established by the show of public authority, which is considered as the representative of the whole people, then they are accounted laws."

The master-workman who in the middle ages employed but two or three apprentices and as many journeymen, gave way to a class of capitalists, enriched by the confiscated wealth of the church, by the treasures imported from America and the Indies, and by the profits of the slave-traffic, who at once prepared to take advantage of the stimulus to industry given by the opening of a vast world market. As late as the middle of the last century, however, manufacturing was still carried on by masters who employed but a small number of hands, and had but little capital invested in the business; and the modern industrial era, with its factory system, properly begins with our marvellous mechanical inventions and the use of steam as a motive power. Machinery made production on a large scale possible, and threw the whole business into the hands of capitalists, while laborers are left with nothing but their ability to work, which they are forced to sell at whatever price it will bring. The capitalist's one aim is to amass wealth, and he buys human labor just as he buys machinery or raw material, at the lowest rate at which it can be obtained. It is either denied that the question of wages has an ethical aspect, or it is maintained that the competition among capitalists themselves, which under the present system of production is inevitable, compels employers to ignore considerations of equity. Hence it comes to be held that what-

ever increases profits is right. The hours of
labor are prolonged, the sexes are intermingled,
children are put to work in factories, sanitary
laws are violated; wares are made in excess of
demand; and, in consequence of the resulting
glut of the markets, wages are still further lowered or work is stopped; and the laborers,
whether they continue to work or whether they
strike, or are forced into idleness, are threatened with physical and moral ruin. The further development of the system is, in the opinion
of many observers, towards the concentration
of capital in immense joint-stock companies and
syndicates, whose directors, by buying compet-
ing concerns and also legislatures and judges,
make opposition impossible, and render the condition of laborers still more hopeless.

This brief sketch of the history and nature
of industrialism is sufficient to account for the
existence of the various socialistic theories and
movements of the present day. The word Socialism, which first came into use in the early
part of the nineteenth century, stands rather for
a tendency than for a definite body of principles
and methods, and this tendency is one of which
men of very different and even opposite opinions approve: and a Socialist may be a theist
or an atheist, a spiritualist or a materialist, a
Christian or an agnostic. The general impli-

cation is the need of greater equality in the condition of human beings. The aim, therefore, is to bring about a social arrangement in which all will receive a fair share of the good things of life; and the best way to secure this, Socialists commonly think, is to render the will of the individual more completely subordinate to that of the community. The methods by which this may · be accomplished are not necessarily violent or revolutionary. In the opinion of many serious writers, Socialism is the logical outcome of tendencies which are held to prevail throughout the civilized world. Our views of liberty, equality, and fraternity, they say, must necessarily lead not merely to the reign of the people, to a universal democracy, but must embody themselves in a State which will own both land and capital, and will control both production and distribution; for only in this way can all be made free and equal, and the brotherhood of the race become something better than ironical cant. Already the State has widened its sphere of action. It has passed laws to regulate industry, it has taken charge of education, and there are many indications that the tendency is to assume that whatever concerns the health, happiness, and morals of the people should be subject to State control. The massing of capital in great corporations is the beginning of a movement, it is thought, which will end in the transference of all capital to the one sole corporate State. The different labor unions and coöperative societies are regarded as schools in which the working classes are receiving the education needed to prepare them for the task of universal intelligent coöperation. The Socialists hold, also, that the moral progress of the modern world. points in the same direction. There is a wider sympathy, a new sense of justice, a desire to come to the help of the weak and wronged, a consciousness of the responsibility, not of individuals alone but of society, which must lead to a readjustment of the social order in accordance with the sentiments of the more humane temper which is characteristic of our age. And is not all this, in part at least, a result of the teaching and example of Christ himself, who came to preach the Gospel to the poor, to heal the infirm and to bring relief to the overburdened, and who thus gave the impulse which has finally developed into our humanitarian faith, hope, and love? A large number of Socialists, it is true, are atheists and materialists, but the earnest desire to discover some means whereby justice may be done the people, whereby they may be relieved from their poverty and misery, and the resulting vice and crime, is in intimate harmony with the gentle and loving spirit of Him who passed no sorrow by.

From the general principle that it is the duty of the rich and strong to use at least part of their wealth and strength in the service of their fellow-men, and first of all in the service of the poor and helpless, no good or wise man will dissent. Here, then, is a common ground whereon all, whatever their philosophic and religious opinions and beliefs may be, can meet. Disagreement arises only when we come to discuss how this may best be done. If, however, the discussion is to be useful, it is necessary that we first get a true view of the condition of the classes to whose relief we wish to come.

Are the evils from which they suffer really as great and desperate as the Socialist agitators would have us believe? Are laborers worse paid, worse fed, worse clothed, and worse housed than, for instance, in the early part of the nineteenth century? Do they labor a greater number of hours, and is their work more severe and exhausting now than then?

Is the tendency of present conditions to make them unintelligent, brutal, and reckless? Is the actual economic system an organization of the ruling classes to keep the laborers in poverty and permanent subjection? Is it a fact, in a word, that we are drifting towards a state of things in which the few shall own everything and the many nothing?

If these questions are to receive an affirmative answer, then the method of production by private competitive capital should be condemned, for it not only, in this case, works injustice to large multitudes, but must, if permitted to continue in operation, finally lead to social ruin. It is easily intelligible that those who believe that private capitalism is essentially vicious, should look to Socialism as a ground for hope, and that they should find in the supposed tendencies of the present economic developments a reason for thinking that the reign of individualism is nearing its end.

The democracy, upon which light is streaming from many sources, which all the forces and struggles of society are helping to organize more thoroughly, and which is rapidly becoming conscious of its superior power, could not be expected to accept as permanent a system which makes of the mass of the people a herd of proletarians, dependent upon uncertain wage-labor.   Already, under democratic influence, the State has assumed functions formerly performed by individuals, families, and minor communities, and under the pressure of the growing sense of the responsibility of society for the welfare of all its members, it tends to widen the sphere of its activity and to take greater control of the lives of citizens.

And as it always happens when the stream of tendency sets strongly in a given direction, those who oppose not less than those who favor hasten the coming of the new order. Events, in fact, solve the great problems, and our discussions are but the foam that crests the waves. Thus, it is conceivable that the efforts of competitive capital to save itself by forming colossal companies and syndicates, may be found in the end to facilitate the transference of the whole to the collective management of society.

The era of the small producer, it is plain, has passed away. Indeed, the greatest sufferers among laborers, at present, are the victims of what is known as the Sweating System, which is an unhealthy survival of the method of domestic production. If the choice, then, is between the massing of capital in a few hands and its complete control by the State, there can be little doubt as to what the final decision will be.

But the question whether the Socialist view of the actual condition of labor and of the tendencies of the present economic order, is the true view, still remains to be answered.

There are reasons which should lead us to

look upon the assertions of the Socialist agitators with a certain distrust. The temper of reformers is enthusiastic, and hence they almost inevitably exaggerate the evils they seek to correct. The crowd is fond of reckless statement, and its leaders not unfrequently win and hold their preëminence by the boldness with which they deal in passionate rhetoric. It is well known, too, that when patients begin to improve they become irritable; and this is true also of suffering bodies of men. The hopeless become resigned. The negro slaves began and ended the day's work to the sound of their own melodies; and when women were treated like slaves the indignities they suffered called forth no clamorous protests. The discontent and agitation which now exist among the working classes are not, then, a proof that their condition is altogether evil or that it is growing worse, while the testimony of the leaders in the labor-movements is, for the reasons I have given, open to suspicion.

No enlightened mind doubts the superiority of our civilization to that of all preceding centuries, and yet when was there ever so much fault-finding as now with the evils and shortcomings of political, social, and domestic life?

We have even a literature which proclaims that life itself is worthless; and there are evidently a number of readers who are interested in arguments which go to show that marriage, free institutions, popular education, civilization, and Christianity have all broken down and failed to bring the good they promised and which the human heart craves.

Our gains seem to have served only to make us more conscious of what we still lack, and in the light of our intellectual, moral, and material progress we easily persuade ourselves that what has been achieved is little more than the promise of better things to be. Then our implements of almost magical power and delicacy, and the ease and rapidity with which by their aid we are able to overcome mere physical obstacles, have made us impatient. We rebel against the teaching which inculcates the wisdom of making haste slowly, and we imagine that by teaching people to read and write, and by proper legislative enactments, we may do away with ignorance, poverty, and crime as easily as we drain swamps or recover exhausted soil. In this our temper is unphilosophic and misleading. Social development depends upon laws which legislation can modify only to a limited extent, and a prerequisite to all effective and desirable social transformations is a corresponding change in the character of both the masses and their rulers and em-

ployers. Now, alterations in the character of
a people are the result of slow processes, carried on through successive generations, and
hence it is a mistake to suppose that a change
in the machinery of government will suddenly
produce an equivalent change in the thought
and conduct of men. The futility of mere
paper constitutions has been proven by experi-
ments which leave no room for doubt. Mexico,
for example, has had republican institutions
since the early part of this century, but the
condition of the masses of its people is little
better than was that of the slaves in the South-
ern States.

Putting aside, then, as impracticable all
schemes for bringing on an era of universal
comfort and contentment by mechanical changes
in the constitution of society, let us strive to
get a clear view of the results and tendencies
of the actually existing system of competitive
capitalistic production.

In the first place, it is a fact that, neither in
Europe nor in the United States, is there a
chasm between the enormously rich and the
very poor, but there is a gradation of possession from the beggar to the great capitalist.
Most of what is said about the poverty and
misery of the working class is applicable only
to what has been called the social residuum,

which may be compared to the stragglers and
camp-followers of an army; and the social
gulf is not between rich men and steady, thrifty
laborers, but rather between these latter and the
crowd of loafers and criminals. That the cause
of this disparity of condition is moral rather
than economic, whoever observes may see; and
this fact gives emphasis to the great truth that
all real amelioration in the lot of human beings
depends on religious, moral, and intellectual
conditions. Money does not make a miser rich
nor its lack a true man poor. The most com-
petent authorities, basing their opinion upon
exhaustive statistical study and careful obser-
vation, hold that the condition of laborers
during the industrial period has been one of
gradual improvement. In England, from 1688
to 1800, there was an increase of less than fifty
per cent in the number of laborers, and an increase of six hundred and ten per cent in their
total earnings; and from 1800 to 1883 workers
increased a little over four hundred per cent
and their income about six hundred per cent.
Wages have risen both in amount and in pur-
chasing power. The hours of labor have become fewer and the rate of mortality has
decreased. " Taken as a whole," says Professor Levi, who is a recognized authority on
questions of statistics, " the working classes of

the United Kingdom may be said to be stronger
in physique, better educated, with more time at
their command, in the enjoyment of greater
political rights, in a more healthful relation
towards their employers, receiving higher wages
and better able to effect some savings, in 1884
than they were in 1857." And in England the
conditions are less favorable to the laboring
classes than in some other countries, far less
favorable than they are in our own. It is
densely populated; it imports much of its food;
nearly all the land is owned by a few thousand
families; its workmen have been crippled and
dwarfed by laws made in the interest of employers; and production and distribution are
regulated according to the principles of free
trade, which we here in America, at least, are
taught to believe has a tendency to lower
wages.

In the United States, it is plain, there is no
gulf between the very rich and the very poor,
but a gradation of widely distributed wealth.
More than eight million families are land-
owners, and of the thirteen million families
among whom the wealth of the country is divided, eleven million families are said to belong
to the wage-earning class. We have, indeed, a
few enormously rich men, but it will be found
difficult to hold these great fortunes together,

and if plutocrats should persist in abusing the power which money gives, the people will know how to protect themselves against the tyrants.

If private property is not a crime, and that it is not even radical Socialists admit, then wealth however great, if it be honestly acquired and justly used, must be respected. Much of the material progress of our country is due to the energy and foresight of men who, if they have grown rich themselves, have made possible the comfortable and independent existence of thousands. Diatribes against wealthy men oftener spring from unworthy passions than from any sense of wrongs inflicted by them. Duties and responsibilities are personal, and the poor are bound not less than the rich to do what they are able to promote the common welfare. The obligation of service is universal, and to encourage jealousy and hatred of the rich among the poor is to do harm to the interests and character of both. If the rich are sometimes selfish and heartless, they are quite as often generous and helpful. Like other men, they are conscious of the irresistible leaning of human nature to the side of justice, and if a sort of all-embracing good-will is characteristic of Americans, we may hope that all efforts to cause class-hatred to prevail here will

prove futile. At all events, the condition of
laborers under the *régime* of competitive production, whatever grievances they still may
have, are not so desperate as to make us willing to run the risk of putting in jeopardy the
two things we have learned to value the most
-- Liberty and Individuality.

Many of our social arrangements are doubtless provisional only. In various ways our age
is transitional, and such an age is necessarily
one of exceptional hardship for the weak; but
in an era of change the last thing the wise will
counsel is the rushing into visionary and un-
tried schemes of reform; and such a scheme,
where there is question of a whole people, the
New Socialism certainly is. In small communities even the Socialist theory has been found
impracticable except where celibacy has been
made a condition of membership. The social
order is an organism infinitely complex, the
outcome of many forces, whose action and in-
teraction, beginning in the obscure and mysterious regions where life and mind first manifest
themselves, have been going on for unnumbered ages; and it has so intertwined itself
with man's very nature that we may say he is
what he is in virtue of the society of which he
is the product. By it our language, our literature, our laws, and much of our religion have

been developed. To make desirable, or possible even, a radical change in this order, such as that implied by Socialism, our nature itself would have to become other. Until this changes, man will continue to believe that he has the right to own property, and he will continue to look upon the possession of a home and of other things whereby an independent existence for himself and his wife and children is secured, as among the chief boons of life. The owner of the poorest cabin would not barter it for the promises of the Socialist paradise. The passion for independence, for liberty, which, inborn in our portion, at least, of the Aryan race, has been strengthened and intensified by centuries of heroic struggles, makes us averse to social schemes which, if practical at all, can succeed only by controlling and regulating all the affairs of life, by turning the whole nation into an industrial army, where each one is under orders to keep the place and do the duties assigned him. There is nothing we so much dislike as interference — we who think it better to be insulted than to have even advice proffered. In America we know our politicians too well to be able to believe that captains of industry, under the control of a supreme council, to whom power vastly greater than that which politicians and bosses have ever exercised would necessarily be given in a Socialist government, could safely or wisely be entrusted with the management of all our nearest and dearest concerns.

If, indeed, the root-principle of the New Socialism, as set forth by Marx, and before him by Ricardo, — that labor is the sole source of value, and that therefore capital is robbery, — were true, it would certainly be a powerful argument against the existing economic order, and would drive honest men to look with approval upon projects to substitute in its place some method of production and distribution which would not be in open conflict with the current ideas of morality. Neither religion nor humanity permits us to acquiesce in a system of organized plunder, and if this is what competitive capitalism is, the transformation of society, by revolution if need be, is an end for which all good men might well labor. If we assume, with the school of Ricardo, that all wealth, all exchange value, is the result exclusively of labor, then to the laborers all wealth rightfully belongs, and capitalists have acquired what they possess by the spoliation of the true owners; and the collectivism of Marx, who proposes to turn all land and capital over to the State, which undertakes to pay every one the full worth of his work, is a logical development.

Political economists, however, now generally agree in holding that the theory of Ricardo, which makes labor the only source of value, is untenable; for capital, which is required for production, must be accepted as a factor in determining values, and its owner therefore is entitled to a fair reward for the service his capital renders. It may be said that capital itself is the result of labor, but it must be admitted that it is also the result of abstinence from consumption. While one man consumes the equivalent of his entire work, another consumes but part, and thus gradually accumulates a capital, which he invests in some machine, for instance, and thereby acquires a right to whatever value the machine may add to manufactured products. His machine has become his fellow-laborer, and if large and perfect enough, will do the work of many men. What right can the State have to take from him this labor-saving instrument, which he has invented or paid for with money honestly earned?

The fallacy of the Socialist assumption lies in attributing to labor a value of its own, independently of the worth of its product. The labor spent in doing useless things has no value; at least, no social value. He who makes what nobody wants has his labor for his pains. The question is not what amount of labor an object

has cost, but what service can it render. A
man may devote years to learning to walk the
tight-rope, but if I do not care for such attain-
ments and exhibitions, I will not pay to see
him perform.   Values, then, cannot be esti-
mated in terms of labor, which is nevertheless
the task the Socialists have set themselves.
How shall we determine the worth of the labor
expended in perfecting a plan such as that which
led Columbus to discover America?   What is
the worth of Newton's labor in evolving the
theory of gravitation, of Shakspere's in writing
" Hamlet," of Wagner's in composing " Parsi-
fal," of Gutenberg's in making his type, or of
Watt's in building his steam-engine?   Without
the genius of inventors and discoverers, without
the foresight and enterprise of investors and
capitalists, there would be little for laborers to
do, and society would drift into general poverty.

Far, then, from being the sole source of value,
labor, to have worth, must be provided with the
raw materials and forces of nature; must be
stimulated and directed by intelligence, and must
produce things which human beings want; and
capital, which is not so much the result of labor
as of abstinence from consumption, which leaves
a surplus of the labor product to be invested in
profit-bearing enterprises, necessarily shares also
in the determination of values.   The present

economical system, then, is not, as Socialists affirm, organized injustice, though it must be admitted that it often leads to wrongs which cripple the lives of multitudes, and produce an incalculable amount of physical and moral evil. Indeed, the present inequalities in the distribution of wealth affect the moral sense so painfully that we cannot look upon them as irremovable. We may not, however, trample on rights to secure greater distributive justice, or approve of schemes which if they promise a greater abundance of material things to the poor, would lead to a general enfeeblement and lowering of human life. In a Socialist State, in which the universal ideal is that of physical well-being and comfort, the sublimer moods which make saints, heroes, and men of genius possible would no longer be called forth. If all should receive the same reward, whatever their labor, spontaneity would come to an end and progress cease, and such an equality would finally come to be a universal equality in indolence, poverty, and low thinking; while from an ethical point of view, it would seem to be unjust that the same reward should be given to every kind of labor.

If different rewards are given for different kinds of work, the practical difficulties in determining the social value of the different kinds of labor appear to be insuperable, especially when we consider that in the Socialist State there are to be no special payments, no money to serve as a universal standard of value. What shall be the basis of comparison for fixing the relative value of the work of a carpenter, a nurse-maid, a schoolmaster, and a minister of religion? If it be said that each shall receive according to the amount and social utility of his or her productive labor, how is this rule to be applied? Every product is the result of the operation of many forces, natural, mechanical, and human, and to decide what part of the value is due to the labor of any special workman is extremely difficult, if not impossible. If we accept the formula, " To each in proportion to the number of hours of his work," which is said to be in the strictest sense the theoretical basis of Socialism, then skilled and unskilled labor will be paid alike; and since the acquirement of skill is the result of long and painful processes, who would take infinite pains when by so doing he would gain nothing? And how shall we apply this time-measure to agricultural labor, to domestic service, to woman's work in the family, where she has at once the offices of wife, mother, nurse, and housekeeper? If skilled labor receives a greater reward than the unskilled the principle of equality is aban-

doned, while the relative values of the two kinds
of labor must be arbitrarily assumed.

Not only, then, is the Socialist theory of the
source of value unsatisfactory, but the methods
by which it is proposed to bring about a more
equal distribution of wealth are either impracticable or, if applied, would lead to greater evils
than those from which we actually suffer.
There would, indeed, have to be a radical change
in man's moral nature before it would be safe
to entrust to any body of men such power as
the managers of the Socialist State would inevitably acquire. It is with power as with
money — those who love it never have enough;
and in fact if the whole economic management
of society, together with the education of the
young, were turned over to a special governing
and directing class, its power would necessarily
have to be almost unlimited. The whole people
would be marshalled like an army, and unques-
tioning obedience would be demanded and enforced. The right of the people to elect their
officers gives no assurance that their favorites
will be worthy or capable. What universal suf-
frage does to bring the best and the wisest into
power is now well known. The policy and the
candidates of the people are the policy and the
candidates of wire-pullers and bosses. They
who should once get hold of the vast and com-

plex machinery by which it is proposed to govern the Socialist State would most probably remain in power; and when we reflect that all the printing-presses of the country would be under their control, and that there would be no reason for the existence of political parties, it is difficult to see how they could be driven from office. The selfishness which, under the *régime* of competitive capitalism, makes so many employers of labor heartless and tyrannical, would assert itself also in the new order; for a change of government is like a change of clothes, it leaves the man what he was. It is incredible that the perversity of human passion may be corrected by mechanical appliances. Its source lies within, where lie also the aids to noble life; and until there is a universal change of heart, a social theory which assumes that every man loves all men as much as he loves himself is utopian. Observant minds belonging to different schools of thought agree in holding that in the modern world egotism is more intense than it was in the middle ages, at least so far as there is question of the love of money, which now is the form all our selfish passions naturally take; for money means power, it means self-indulgence, it means the satisfaction of vanity, it means honor and place. Mere intellectual training is powerless to correct this vice or to bring about any great moral improvement. It tends to change the form of vice rather than to make us virtuous; or, if we should take a more hopeful view of what secular education is able to do, the time is certainly distant when the masses can be called educated, in any real sense of the word.

Though we cannot accept the fundamental principles of Socialism or Collectivism as true, and though we are persuaded that society cannot successfully be established upon them as a basis, there are none the less bonds of sympathy between us and the Socialists. The desire, which in the case of many of them is doubtless earnest and sincere, to come to the relief of the poor, to find some means by which their lot may be made less miserable, springs from a divine impulse. It is Christian and human; and the anti-religious spirit of modern Socialism comes from an unphilosophic and unhistoric view of the forces which create civilization and give promise of a better future. Atheism and materialism fatally strengthen and intensify man's selfish passions, by merging life's whole significance and worth into the present transitory existence. If there is no order of absolute truth and right, no future for the individual, then pleasure is the chief good, and both instinct and reason impel to indulgence and to the overthrow of society, if society makes the enjoyment of life impossible. Hence the socialism of materialists and atheists logically leads to anarchy. Nothing could be more sad than that the multitude should be driven to look for deliverance from their wrongs and sorrows to leaders who deny God, and man's kinship with the infinitely true and perfect One; who tell them that there is no living heavenly Father, but only an unconscious Earth-Mother, on whose senseless body Life and Death play their horrid farce. The grasping avarice and heartless methods of employers and capitalists, who generally profess to be Christians, are arguments against religion which the preachers of atheism find effective in addressing the victims of our present economic system; while the decay of faith has greatly diminished the persuasive force of appeals in favor of resignation and submission. Those who lose faith and hope and love, lose patience too; and it is futile to preach the sacredness of wealth to the poor when their miserable lives are the sad witnesses to the immorality of the means by which it is acquired.

Who can read the history of rack-renting in Ireland, or the story of the Sweating System in the "Bitter Cry of Outcast London," without feeling that a social order which makes such things possible ought to be changed or destroyed?

Who can consider the mental, moral, and physical state of certain classes of emigrants who land upon our shores by the thousand, without asking ourselves whether the countries from which these people come are civilized and Christian? Has the passion for humanity which Christ came to inspire, and which was a living principle in his early followers, died in Christian Europe? There the very poor certainly are excluded from our spiritual and material inheritance, and it would seem that the standing armies which are kept up by the various powers are maintained rather for the purpose of holding the impoverished masses in subjection than for defence against foreign aggression. It is as though the ruling classes in Europe had entered into a conspiracy to foment national jealousy and hatred, that they may have a pretext for keeping intact their military organizations, which, while they overawe the people, help to reduce them to still greater poverty and wretchedness. There Socialism may have a meaning, and since there are never wanting with us people who think it the proper thing to take whatever infection may prevail in Europe, it was inevitable that certain dilettants and idiosyncratics should seek to persuade us that America too ought to have its Socialism. We began, however, as the most completely individualist people of which history makes record, and our experience has not tended to weaken our faith in the power of freedom, intelligence, and industry to solve the great social problems. Should our plutocrats, instead of making themselves public benefactors, become public malefactors, a modification in the laws of inheritance, together with other legal measures which would readily suggest themselves, would be sufficient to abate the nuisance. For the rest, we are convinced that the great aim should be not to provide for all men, but to train and educate all men to take care of themselves. The tendency of good government is to make government less necessary, and the influence of the religion of Christ not only creates purer morals and sympathies, but it also mitigates the conflict between the Church and the world.

As men become more enlightened and human, they perceive that the aims of the best civil government are not really distinct from those of true religion. Man's salvation here and hereafter is the end for which all society exists, and hence it is the duty both of the Church and the State to labor for freedom, knowledge, and righteousness; in other words, for humanity. The nineteen centuries which have passed since Christ was born have put new forces into our hands, which, if we but use them with wisdom

and in the spirit of Christian love, may teach
that the Saviour came not to redeem the individual alone, but to transform society. We
have at our disposal the vast treasure of science,
which is ever increasing, and which, if we but
have understanding and a heart, may be made
to bless alike the rich and the poor with greater
knowledge of the causes of physical evil, of
hygienic and sanitary laws, which shall become
more and more able to forestall disease. We
shall make education universal, but we shall
educate with a view to health of body and soul
quite as much, at least, as with a view to sharpen
the mental faculties. We shall gradually come
to understand that there is no conflict between
religion and science, but that both are mani-
festations of God's wisdom and love, meant to
console, strengthen, and save man. The minister of religion will love knowledge and the
man of science will be reverent and devout.
When coöperation becomes universal not among
laborers alone, but when the men of wealth
and the men of toil, the men of religion and
the men of science, the spiritual guides and
the temporal rulers, all unite for the common
good of the whole people, a new era will dawn.
All will then recognize that intelligence and
morality are the basis of human life; and that
as right intelligence leads to faith in God, so is

that faith the fountain-head of the generous and fervid moods which make righteousness prevail.   We shall understand more thoroughly that the causes of vice and crime are the chief causes also of poverty and all other social evils.

And while this truer view will weaken confidence in the mechanical appliances and patent remedies of reformers and empirics, it will confirm our faith in the efficacy of pure religion, of right education, and of whatever else nourishes and strengthens the faculties within.

Then shall a more perfect society grow round us — a society complex and various, yet free and orderly, rich in art, vocal in literature, strong in sympathy, victorious through the power of holiness and love.

II.

THE BASIS OF POPULAR GOVERNMENT.

FENELON spoke from his generous heart when he said, "I love my family more than myself, my country more than my family, and the whole world more than my country." Unfortunately, the converse of this is true of men in general, who love themselves first, their families next, then their country, and the whole world hardly at all. Hence the inefficacy of arguments intended to show that abuses in which an age takes delight will bring harm to posterity. Those who prefer the lower to the higher self will make no sacrifices for the good of their descendants, as one who is indifferent to the living will surely be unmindful of the dead and the unborn. We care nothing for ancestors who are a few degrees removed from us, unless their lives furnish food to our vanity, and it is not probable that any man is made unhappy by pondering on the destiny that may await his great-grandchildren. Declaimers against the evils of the age, who predict the

3

not distant downfall of the State or of civilization, alarm no one, because few have faith in such forebodings, and fewer still care to trouble themselves about the condition of mankind a hundred years hence. The masses of Europeans and Americans are little concerned for the welfare of the populations of Africa and eastern Asia; they are too far away. And time separates even more than space.

Here in America, to within a quite recent date, we have been so wholly under the influence of unreasoning optimism and youthful self-complacency, that prophets of evil have appeared to us to be simply men of unsound mind. As a people we have been, and probably still are, believers in the fundamental error that denies the original taint in man's nature; and hence we are persuaded that, in a society like ours, where the restraints, oppressions, and injustices of past ages have ceased to exist, the tendency to higher modes of thought and conduct, to purer and worthier life, is as irresistible as the laws of nature. The enthusiasm with which men hailed the advent of the rule of the people, and the promise of boundless good to the race with which the new order of things was ushered in, together with a knowledge of the terrible and indescribable evils that unjust laws and tyrannical governments have brought

upon mankind, were sufficient to blind them to
the common facts of personal experience, and
to hide from philosophers a truth known to
every mother and every nurse, that man is born
not only weak and ignorant, but with such a
tendency to what is vicious that each generation of children, if left to the impulse of their
will, would inevitably relapse into barbarism.

The bent of human nature is toward what
is beneath, and the natural course of society
is downward. If we consider the history of
our race, we find emergence from barbarism
to be the fortunate lot of exceptional people,
who by some divine impulse are borne upward,
and, having reached a certain height of civilization, hasten to descend, not, indeed, along
the rugged paths of heroic daring and self-
denial by which they mounted the summit, but
in the open and easy way of sensual delights.
Among the most privileged nations, only the
smallest number attain to excellence, and their
high endowments, whether moral or intellectual, depend upon unceasing effort. The great
body of their fellow-countrymen are held to be
civilized on account of their association with
these better specimens of the race, just as a
vulgar man is called noble because he descends
from ancestors who are believed to have been
really so. Few men love the best, or seek the

highest, or strive to shape their lives upon the model of exalted ideals; and the truly excellent, whether in conduct, literature, or art, is never popular. The crowd neither follow in the footsteps of the noblest characters, nor read the best books, nor love the master-works of genius. It may, indeed, be said to be a law of human nature that attraction from below is stronger than attraction from above. The multitude live in the senses, not in the soul; and the life of the senses is contact with material objects. Hence the fatal tendency to superficial views of life and to low notions of conduct. How long and patiently must not a man labor to bring his natural endowments to some kind of perfection? And the moment he ceases to toil marks the beginning of degeneracy. But this tireless struggle is hard to weak nature, and the multitudes yield to the current, and are carried farther and farther away from the heights their young eyes looked up to with hope, all aglow with the light of ideal worlds. The same law prevails in families. But very few rise to eminence, and they, having produced two or three men of mark, break up and are lost in obscurity.

It is difficult to understand why we should imagine that there is in human nature a principle of indefinite progress. There is, indeed, in the world to-day more knowledge than there has ever been, more wealth, more comfort, more liberty; but, apart from the fact that all this is in great measure attributable to the influence of Christianity, which was accepted as a supernatural faith, supplying supernatural motives and helps, the essential quality of human life lies elsewhere than in knowledge, wealth, comfort, and liberty. Men and nations fail, not for lack of these, but for lack of moral strength. Conduct, to use a current phrase, is three-fourths or four-fifths of human life; and man is to such an extent a moral being that failure in conduct is essential, hopeless failure. The sense of life, of its goodness, its joyousness, its inestimable worth, springs from right-doing, not from fine thinking, or the enjoyment of political freedom, or the possession of wealth. Pure hearts are glad, and they who tread the paths of duty find God's world sweet. This is not a theory, but a truth that all men may verify by actual experiment, and to it the unvarying testimony of the past bears witness. That moral life is joy, peace, gladness, contentment, fullness of life, is the teaching of all the greatest thinkers of the world; and it is also the actual experience of every human being who walks obedient to the voice of God's stern daughter, Duty. This is not to say that right-doing necessarily makes people happy, but that it gives them a deeper sense of the value of life and of its sacredness, a better insight into the goodness of all things, a knowledge that evil is accidental, and in no way able to deprive man of the blessedness that comes of being in conscious harmony with the eternal laws of God's universe. To be morally right is to be absolutely right, because the infinite truth of what is, is more nearly revealed to the conscience than to the intellect; and the more closely we conform to the law within, the more God-like does the whole world external to ourselves grow to be. In this way moral excellence, awakening the deep and boundless harmonies that sleep within the soul, brings us near to the heart of love and creates faith in immortal life. When character is the result of conformity with eternal laws, we feel that this union is everlastingly true, good, and fair; and hence that our real self belongs to an order of things that is imperishable. Therefore the good are strong, and so, happy, since weakness is misery.

Just as right-doing leads to completeness of life and to belief in life everlasting, so wrong-doing begets a dis-esteem of life and unbelief in man's God-like destiny. " Let us eat and drink, for to-morrow we die," are the words of those who fail in conduct. The more we live in the senses, the less becomes our faith in the value and duration of life. Hence the reckless-ness of those who have thrown aside moral re-straint, and the fatal facility with which they take their own and others' lives. Thought, to be true and healthful, must complete itself in act. It is not, therefore, its own end, but aims at something beyond. In the same way faith, hope, and love tend to action, to morality, to righteousness; and thus from all sides the truth is borne in upon us that the test of human worth is to be found in character, and not in a culti-vated mind, or a brilliant imagination, or in beauty of body, and much less, of course, in things that are purely material, as money and machinery. Progress, then, is not possible where there is moral decadence, since conduct is three-fourths of life, and character the real test of man's worth. The literary excellence and refined civilization of the age of Augustus and of the age of Louis XIV. were not only wholly powerless to arrest the decay of Roman and French society, but served rather to hasten its dissolution; and history testifies to the truth that the possession of wealth destroys the vir-tues by which it is created.

If we turn to our own country, and to what, unfortunately, we must still call an experiment, to determine whether the best possible kind of government may become an enduring fact, we cannot fail to perceive that, to be able to form an enlightened opinion as to the success or failure of this noblest effort at self-government ever made by mankind, the truth that I have here sought to develop must be borne in mind. Human worth is moral worth; man's proper measure is character; conduct is three-fourths of life; right-doing brings the deepest and most lasting content and gladness to the heart of man, and thus creates a sense of completeness and harmony that nothing else can give. Righteousness is strength. As the physical forces of the boundless universe work together in every drop of water to give and maintain its form and nature, so the infinite power that makes goodness the best, coöperates with every man who obeys conscience, to uphold and confirm his heart. Goodness of life tends to length of days, to health, to success. Man lives by faith, hope, and love; and fidelity to conscience keeps him close to the clear-flowing fountain-head of faith, hope, and love. To think finely is well; to dream nobly is also good; and to look with a glad heart upon the beauties of the universe gives delight; but not in doing any of these things, but in doing right, lies the worth and goodness of life. And this great principle affects families and nations as it affects individuals. Conduct leads a whole people along the rugged and difficult ascent of progress; and, without it, neither knowledge, nor wealth, nor numbers, nor machinery, nor fertile soil, nor healthful climate, nor all these together, with whatever else there may be that is good and helpful, can save them from decadence and ruin. Whether alone or one of a multitude, man fails not for lack of anything else than virtue.

That a democratic form of government ought to be the best, the proverb, " If you wish a thing done, do it yourself," would seem sufficiently to prove. Again: Since the end of government is to promote the welfare of all the governed, and since each man is more than any one else interested in his own behalf, and since interest in a subject or a cause awakens attention and begets intelligence in matters therewith connected, it would seem to follow that to give to all men a due degree of influence in the government is the surest way to promote the welfare of all. And this conclusion gains weight when we reflect that whoever hopes more from his own industry and merit than from fortune and favor is a natural republican. On the other hand, there seems to be no doubt that the government of the best men is really the best government;

and, since this is so, that a democratic government, where the people are corrupt, is necessarily a bad government, because the vicious will not only not elect the best, who will not stoop to their level, but, by virtue of the law of affinity, will choose the baser sort of men. It was this kind of democracy that repelled Landor, — " Because," said he, " I have always found it more jealous of merit, more suspicious of wisdom, more proud of riding on great minds, more pleased at raising up little ones above them, more fond of loud talking, more impatient of calm reasoning, more unsteady, more ungrateful, and more ferocious; above all, because it leads to despotism through fraudulence, intemperance, and corruption."

·As the liberty of criminals means license, so the freedom of the immoral means corruption. Declaimers are fond of affirming that man naturally loves liberty, when the truth is, he only naturally hates restraint. Liberty is obedience to law; and is it not absurd to assert that men are naturally obedient to law, when religion, education, civil authority, criminal codes, and other means have to be continually employed to enforce respect for authority? Do savages, barbarians, and children love the moral restraint without which it is not possible even to think of liberty? Have not men in all ages called liberty the opportunity to seek their own interests and gratify their passions by inflicting wrongs upon their fellow-beings? All virtue is rare, but love of liberty is a virtue, the flower and fruit of a life-long devotion to rectitude, to unselfish purposes and aims as large as the love of Christ. Let us not imagine, then, that a free government such as ours rests upon the natural instincts of the human heart. We love the highest when we see it, but the low cannot see the highest, and only the best know the best.

Our great good fortune lies in our infinite wealth of opportunity. Whoever feels within himself force of mind or heart or body, finds work to do that brings reward; and as he moves forward, avenues open out at every step that lead or promise to lead to much that men most eagerly desire. Through these thousand channels the flood of energy finds outlets, and catastrophes are avoided. But opportunities diminish with the growth of population and the development of the country; and with the whole world rushing in upon us, we shall soon have to find a way to control destructive agencies which our physical resources and sparse population now render comparatively harmless. We must prepare to meet this emergency. We have seventy-five million people; our wealth is **greater** than that of any other nation; our

machines are the most perfect; and the comforts of life are here within the reach of larger
multitudes of men than have ever enjoyed
them. All this has come like the leaves in
spring-time, and like the fruit in summer; but
numbers do not constitute excellence, and machinery does not fashion souls, and comforts
do not nourish heroes. If the outcome of our
civilization is simply to be the greatest possible
number of well-clad and well-fed human beings,
there is little need of giving serious thought to
such a lubberland of mediocrities; and we may
as well agree with Renan, who thinks us farther removed from true social ideals than any
other people, or with Carlyle, who maintains
that the stupendous feat we have hitherto accomplished is to bring into existence in an in-
credibly short time more millions of bores than
have ever before made earth dismal.

To develop the highest man, and, if it may
be, multitudes of the highest men, is in every
way more desirable than to dig gold or build
railways; and if we are to stand in the van of
all the world, we must have other proofs to
show than our money, our corn, our numbers,
and our machines. " The end of all political
.struggle," says Emerson, " is to establish morality as the basis of all legislation." It is manifest that our politics have become essentially

immoral. Neither party dares to touch any
question that is higher or holier than that of
tariff or no tariff, looking upon a wretched
financial problem as the only vital interest for
a people who lack not money, but virtue. The
eternal principles of justice and morality are
ignored, and our electoral contests have degenerated into mere struggles for office; and to
suggest that conscience ought again to assert
itself in American politics is to make one's self
ridiculous. And all the while the evidences of
moral decadence stare us in the face. There
is the general decay of faith in God and in
the worth of life that is the unfailing mark
of weakening character and sinking morality.
Nothing is longer certain for us but what we
see or touch, so that the whole ideal world,
which is our only true world, is become a
dream; and the young start out in life with no
higher aims than to get money or office. Nothing is left among us that is venerable, or great,
or divine. We look upon God's universe with
the spirit of irreverence in which the author of
" Innocents Abroad " beheld the shrines of religion and art in Europe and Asia. Our smartness renders us incapable of admiration, of
awe, of reverence. We know what the stars
are made of, and think them not more wonderful than an electric light.

The press of our great cities is the chronicle of our life. What does it record? Murders, suicides, robberies, thefts, adulteries, fornications, divorces, drunkenness, gambling, incendiarism, fraudulent bankruptcies, official peculations, with now and then a collision of trains and destruction of life and property by mobs. This fills the news columns. In the editorials we meet with reckless assertion, crude generalization, special pleading, ignorant or dishonest statement of half-truths, insincere praise and lying abuse of public men, frivolous treatment of the highest and holiest subjects — all thrown into that form of false reasoning and loose style which is natural to minds that have not time to learn anything thoroughly. And this half-mental and half-bestial brothel-and-grog mixture, brought from the great cities by special trains to every household, falls like a mildew upon the mind and conscience of the people, taking from them all relish for literature, all belief in virtue, all reverence for God and nature, until one may doubt whether we have not lost the power of intellectual and moral growth.

We have no one institution great enough to inspire the love and enthusiasm that are the soul of national unity. Our public life regards material interests alone; our theory of education is narrow and superficial, aiming chiefly to develop smartness, the least desirable quality of mind, and more sure than any other to foster vulgarity; and thus we have no ideal to elevate and guide us or fill us with faith in our destiny. In the meantime, the manners of Europe threaten us, and we are permitting the rapid growth of social customs that are helpful enough to tyrants, but pernicious in a democratic republic. Austere manners lead to political liberty and uphold free governments; but a people given over to sensual delights, to foolish frolicking and dissipation, love license more than freedom, and, if you but give them wine and a show, care not what master rules over them. The Puritans of New England had the truest instinct of political liberty, and that instinct made them serious, earnest, austere, averse alike to childish gayety and to loose conduct. It were better for us, if our liberty is dear to us, to have the Puritan Sabbath than the Pagan Sunday of parts of Europe. There must be brought into our public life something to appeal to minds and consciences as well as to interests; for it is the disgrace of a nation that its chief concern should be a question of money, and that the significance of political contests should lie in the emoluments of office; and while this state of things continues, the best men will remain aloof from the struggle, and leave the direction of public affairs in the hands of the baser sort. We need an ideal to which all noble minds and generous hearts may rally, and this ideal here in America at the present day can neither be intellectual nor religious; it must be moral. We are too essentially practical to be deeply interested in intellectual truth, and our religious divisions are so various and so far-reaching that a great national regeneration springing from a common faith is not now possible; but there is still left in the mass of the people a deep moral earnestness, which, if it can be called into action, may yet lift the whole nation to higher and purer life. Our two great parties are the principal obstacle in the way of such a movement. It is not possible to arouse the American people thoroughly, except through political agitation, and both these parties — which have become simply mills to grind the people's corn to make bread for office-holders — oppose the whole weight of their organized power to every honest effort to bring about a moral reformation. So long as the multitude is led by them, our worship of majorities will throw an air of quixotism over every attempt to stem the torrent of corruption. The welfare of the nation demands that the one or the other cease to exist; that a new party,

springing from the deep yearning of multitudes
for purer and nobler national life, and upheld
by the enthusiasm inspired by high moral aims
and purposes, may take its place.

We will not here discuss the problems that
the new party will have to solve. They will
relate to moral rather than to material interests. There is, first of all, the question of education. The avoidance of religious teaching in
the common schools has deprived them of moral
influence, and they cultivate a faculty instead of
forming men. Then there is the question of the
liquor traffic. The most hideous phase of our
political life is that which comes of its association with bar-rooms, and the remedy for American pauperism is not a wage or rent theory, but
economy and sobriety. There is, also, the question of woman-suffrage. The experiment will
be made, whatever our theories and prejudices
may be. Women are the most religious, the
most moral, and the most sober portion of the
American people, and it is not easy to understand why their influence in public life is
dreaded. They are the natural educators of
the race, and they and their children are the
chief victims of drunken men; and since men
have been unable or unwilling to form a right
system of education or to find a preventive of
intemperance, there can be no great harm in

4

giving, in these matters at least, an experimental vote to women. Then there is the question of the licentious and obscene press, as unlike a free press as a sot is unlike a true man, which is a more deadly and insidious poison than the adulterated liquor that a deluded people pay for the privilege of drinking.

With us, material interests take care of themselves, since the whole energy of the people turns upon the development of our physical resources; and hence the duty of those who have faith and hope in the destiny of America lies elsewhere. In the presence of a whole people thinking chiefly of money; talking of it, yearning for it, toiling, lying, cheating, to get hold of it; adulterating food and drink to make it; displaying it in all its vulgar glitter in their homes and equipages and on their bodies; discussing and solving all problems, even questions of the soul, from a financial point of view; making money the measure of the value of time; determining the worth of education by the power it develops to amass wealth, and even going so far as to hold a man's money the nearest equivalent of himself, — in the presence of such a people there is need of power to proclaim, as with the voice of God, that the goodness of life lies in right-doing, and not in lucre.

III.

ARE WE IN DANGER OF REVOLUTION?

BATTLES, conflicts, and dangers of all kinds have a mysterious charm for the mind, because life, whether animal, intellectual, or moral, whether individual or social, is developed and attains strength and excellence only through struggle; and it would lose half its charm could we strip it of the element of danger, the risk of loss, the hope of gain, which are never absent where men contend for the mastery. Though victory is the end of fighting, we love the combat more than the victory, and when the battle is won or the game is lost our interest dies; just as the story comes to an end when the fretful stream of love merges into the tame sea of marriage. The objects for which we contend change, but our love of contention never ceases to exist, in spite of the poet's saying that repose is the central feeling of all happiness. Effort, which is born of struggle and conflict, is to life what motion is to water — it keeps it pure and fresh; and an individual or a society which gives over the battle for higher things, fatally sinks to lower plains.

The bloody warfare, which is the delight of savages and barbarians, has ceased to have any charm for the civilized man of the nineteenth century; but he finds himself in the midst of keener and intenser conflicts, from which, if he would live, he cannot escape. Among savages and barbarians the life of the individual is merged and lost in that of the tribe or horde, but, as civilization advances, the individual does not dwindle but grows. The tendency is to enable him to choose his own mode of life and to maintain himself in his position, to break the bonds which hinder the use of his faculties and to send him forth into the arena where the millions contend for wealth or place, and where the better few strive for intellectual and moral superiority. He becomes a reader, a thinker, an independent agent; he helps to mold public opinion and shape the destinies of his fellow-men. In this way civilization brings on the reign of the people, and makes it impossible that any strongest man should control a nation. But the reign of the people in setting mightier forces at work renders more gigantic struggles inevitable. Here in America, freedom of opinion and of conscience has been won; the battle for political and civil liberty has been fought and gained; and other problems present themselves to the human mind which never truly appreciates what it possesses, but by the law of development, as by the hand of God, is led on to new victories. Social questions are now uppermost in men's minds, as political questions absorbed the thought of the eighteenth century. Hereditary privilege has vanished; there is liberty of thought and expression; every man has a right to vote; and still the golden age has not come. Man holds the forces of nature in his hands; by their aid he has increased his wealth to an incredible degree; he has brought the ends of the earth together; and still there are millions who are poor and wretched. Whatever our condition may be as contrasted with that of past ages, the world is still full of evil and discontent. For the first time in their history the Christian nations have created a philosophy of despair, so that it has become possible to doubt whether life itself is not a curse. What numberless patent remedies and panaceas for our troubles have been blazoned forth! The alphabet was to be the key to the garden of Paradise; but the multitude have been taught to read and write, and only clamor the more vociferously that they perish in desert places and quagmires.

Alcohol, it has been asserted, is the supreme

evil; and yet the countless millions of Moham-
medans and Buddhists are sober, but unspeak-
ably wretched. And so each sect raises its cry
affirming or denying, and in the confusion of
tongues reason grows bewildered. God is
solemnly called the Supreme Tyrant, society a
universal crime, property a boundless theft, and
marriage the worst foe of love. All faiths seem
tottering to the verge of shifting opinion, and
in their frenzy many would hardly think it a
loss if the earth itself were shattered. What is
it, anyhow, but an ant-hill lost in space?

Such notions as these find sporadic utterance
here, but they do not represent the thought or
sentiment of any considerable body of Americans. We are not theorists and dreamers, but
workers, who are reasonably satisfied with our
work. This country, it may be said without
incurring the reproach of philistinism, is a
blessed land: nowhere else are such opportunities offered to all men; nowhere else do such
multitudes find it possible to escape from ignorance, poverty, and the impotence of blind
endeavor, into the pure light of free, orderly,
and growing life; nowhere else is there more
general good-will and sympathy in spite of the
mingling of heterogeneous nationalities and
conflicting creeds.

How quickly the angry passions of our Civil

War have sunk to rest, however much demagogues have sought to keep them alive! No
hatred can long flourish here. The poor do not
hate the rich, and the rich as a body are not
indifferent to the wants of the poor. Our
wealthy men are the children of the poor, and
their children or grandchildren will either perish
utterly or go to work again with the laboring
masses. Thus the money line, which is really
the only line with us that separates class from
class, is not a fixed boundary dividing hostile
armies. We have, after all, but a sprinkling
of very rich men, who have their uses, even
when they are unintelligent and narrow-minded,
or personally worthless. Capital is the army
of a commercial age, and capitalists are necessary
to undertake and carry on great enterprises;
they fill the places of the captains of warlike
ages. A railroad king may inflict financial ruin
upon individuals and be unjust to his employees,
but he will develop the country and bring material blessings to thousands. Even stock-
waterers and railway-wreckers probably do
more good than harm to the general public.
But the great capitalists, as I have said, are
few, and in America pauperism is accidental.
The people are neither paupers nor millionaires,
but workers, whose energy and thrift secure
them a competence. Seven million seven hun-

dred and fifty thousand of these are farmers, while only about half that number are engaged in manufacturing. Three-fourths of these farmers own the land they cultivate, and the general tendency is to diminish rather than to increase the size of farms. Our laborers, too, receive higher wages and live in greater plenty than those of any other country. The story of our material progress reads like a dream, and we who are now living see but the beginnings of this incomprehensible work; and in many other respects our course is forward. Each generation begins the life-struggle from a higher plain. The multitudes who arrive here from Europe feel the quickening influence of our life, and their nobler faculties awaken. Thousands each year revisit their native lands and feel like strangers there, so thoroughly have they become imbued with the American spirit. They are not only satisfied with our political institutions, but find it difficult to imagine that they were ever able to bear the shackles and restraints of less liberal governments. If ours is the country of rich men, why do the poor, from the ends of the earth, flock to our shores? If capitalists exercise here a tyrannic power, why do the oppressed of every land seek refuge with us? In truth, we occupy the foremost position among the free nations of the world, and wherever political development is taking place it is in the direction in which we are leading. Our people either know this or feel it instinctively, and they really have no fears at all as to the fortune of the Republic.

There is no other government which rests so completely upon the assent and approval of the governed, and that is the strongest foundation. Shall they who know and feel this grow alarmed because a fanatic has thrown a bomb into a squad of policemen? Or shall they have misgivings as to the future of democratic government because, now and then, here and there, in times of excitement mobs gather and deeds of violence are done? If such things can be a serious danger to the Republic, our condition is indeed pitiable. What peculiar forms of fanaticism may develop in individual cases no one can foresee, but anarchical doctrines must die out here from lack of a suitable environment. They have not sprung from our soil, but have been imported from social conditions wholly dissimilar to ours, and the masses of our laborers have as little sympathy with them as the wealthy classes have. The preaching of such doctrines is undoubtedly criminal, and ought to be punished by law; but our society must undergo radical changes before this fanaticism can become a menace to our institutions. Our politi-

cal life lies in the supremacy of the law, and
any party which attempts to defy its sovereign
majesty will be mercilessly crushed; for the
supremacy of the law means internal peace, the
protection of life and property, and the freedom
of the individual, and it is precisely to secure
these objects that our government exists. A
fanaticism such as that of the anarchists can
grow and extend itself only under an arbitrary
and tyrannical power. Only the sense of the
most terrible wrongs can create so unnatural
and extreme a temper. The destructive tenets
of the Nihilists and German Socialists are the
correlatives of Siberian dungeons and military
despotism; but they cannot become contagious
here, because the food needed for the propagation of the germ is not supplied.

Our labor troubles are of an altogether different nature from this scarecrow of anarchy
and socialism, and they are more serious. It
is our mission to give larger liberty and fuller
life, not to a privileged class but to the whole
people. That the race should live for a few men
is not tolerable from our point of view, and our
destiny compels us to strive to bring about a
social condition in which all men shall live for
every man. Now the lot of the laborer is not
here or anywhere what we know and feel it
might be and ought to be. The laborers, who

in proportion as their minds have been awakened, have become conscious of the hardships and limitations to which they are subject, feel this more keenly than any other class, and hence they have formed innumerable organizations to protect their rights and promote their interests. It is utterly futile to make an outcry against these trades-unions and combinations of unions. They exist, and the ends for which they exist, in spite of incidental abuses connected with their working, are praiseworthy, and there is no power which can put them down.

To attempt to resist or thwart the legitimate claims of working men, is to provoke a state of things which might become a serious menace to the prosperity of the country. The problem is complex, and to look for some easy, ready-made solution is idle. In virtue of a law which is inherent in human nature, the poor are bent upon getting rich, and the rich on growing richer. To get money, and as much money as possible, is the aim and end both of the employer and the employed, and hence there arises between them an inevitable conflict. The capitalist is ready to take advantage of every opportunity to lower wages, the workman of every opportunity to demand higher pay; and thus the almost irresistible tendency is to form themselves into opposing armies, whereas the only hope of a better state of things lies in their being friends. Labor creates capital, and capital gives labor a field to work in.

But of what avail is a truth like this when there is question of controlling passions which are stronger than reason? High and vital principles must be kept in view, and above all, the question must be examined without anger or partisan bias. We should not grow weary of telling rich and poor that there are better things than money; that the best things, as love, virtue, intelligence, cannot be bought; that he whose chief aim in life is to get money and its equivalents is an inferior sort of man; that the truest and the deepest contentment comes of the consciousness of right-doing, and not of the knowledge that we have so many dollars; and that with but little a true man may lead a not unworthy life, and escape the weariness and fears inherent in the possession of riches, which wean the heart from the heavenly fountains of admiration, hope, and love. Truths like these to be effective must be taught by religion and literature, and we who find it impossible to escape the commercial spirit, with its single standard of value, must look to these spiritual powers to give us ideals which may lift us above the flat wastes of materialism. They also alone can properly teach that beauty is useful, that admiration and reverence are essential to noble life, and that to rest in sin or ignorance is the sign of death. Let us also not cease to proclaim that neither God nor churches nor states will save the vicious and the idle from the consequences of their crime and folly; that it is of the nature of right conduct and true work not only to bring success and sufficiency, but to give health, contentment, and strength as well. If the one good is money with what it will buy, then feuds and hatreds must be perpetual. Our wants are infinite, and if you take from man the ideals given by religion and literature, a hundred millions will leave him still a beggar. A false view of life is our radical defect. Our political problems always hinge on some money problem, our educational system looks primarily to the fitting men for money-getting, for our young men success means riches, and our very worship implies that the poor are unfit for the kingdom of heaven. Thus we lose sight of man and think only of money; we increase our wealth, while faith and hope and love and intelligence diminish; we build great cities to be inhabited by little men; we are keen to drive a bargain and slow to recognize a noble soul; we have eyes for bank-notes, and we move dumb and unraised beneath the starlit heavens. If it were possible that a great philosopher or poet should

arise among us, some foreigner would have to
point him out to us; but we know our own, our
men of boundless wealth, whom we envy and
despise. So long as our whole national life-
struggle continues to be carried on around this
single point of finance, what hope is there of
avoiding fatal conflicts? The rich will worship
their god Mammon alone, and the poor will plot
and scheme to shatter the idol; and mechanical
contrivances, such as arbitration boards and
legislative enactments, will leave the root of the
evil untouched.

It is essential that we should know that the
real and final test of a government, as of a religion, is the kind of man it produces, and not
the amount of money. We must return to the
ideals of our forefathers, who preferred freedom, intelligence, and strength to wealth, and
who dedicated this land to higher manhood, and
not to fatter mammonhood. Our politics, our
literature, our whole national life, must be more
concerned for man than for his money. No one
doubts the importance of the interests of trade:
we all desire that our manufacturers should be
able to compete with other nations in the markets
of the world; but if the interests of trade and
competition involve the degradation of millions
of our fellow-citizens, we shall cry out that the
Sabbath was made for man and not man for the

Sabbath. The interests of the working man are primary; the interests of capital are secondary. If the trades-unions shall succeed in forcing politicians to recognize that financial interests are not the only or principal human interests, they will have conferred a benefit upon the nation. Men, and not measures, are the first need of every society, and therefore all social schemes should look first to the forming of true men. But, in truth, only men create and educate men, and one of the delusions of the age is that this can be done by some sort of mechanical contrivance. Hence we look to legislation and government control to do what only vital forces can effect, and after the failure of each enactment some new scheme is tried, until law itself is in danger of falling into discredit. Better laws are desirable, but a true view of life is indispensable, and no state mechanism can properly take care of full-grown men and women who have not learned how to take care of themselves. The growing disposition to look to the general government for aid in every emergency is a symptom of disease; it is an outgrowth of habits and principles contrary to the spirit of our institutions.

The tendency of good government is to make government unnecessary, since it trains people to habits of industry, self-reliance, and order.

The strong and energetic love freedom. A social state in which the whole life of the individual is absorbed and controlled by some external ruling power, can seem good only to the feeble and inactive; and this is the aim of the modern Socialists, and their theories. These have sprung from false and exaggerated sentiment, or from lack of mental soundness and breadth of view, and are a menace to all that is most healthful and manly in human nature and Christian civilization. The end of society is not to secure to all men the highest possible amount of physical comfort and sensual enjoyment, but to give to all men the best possible opportunities of developing their physical, intellectual, moral, and æsthetic endowments; and this is done by stimulating individual energy, and by leaving the highest prizes to be won by effort and struggle. Paternal government is, no doubt, best for children and slaves, but the nobler races have preferred freedom even to the tenderest care.

There is in innumerable minds, who have a horror of the current socialistic doctrines, an unconscious leaning toward socialism, which is seen in the tendency to enlarge the powers of the State. The founders of the Republic held that the State should assume no authority over the individual, save such as is indispensable to

the general welfare; and how far we have de-
parted from this wise and generous view!

The State has taken control of education, and
is thereby weakening one of the most essential
and vital social forces — the sense of responsibility in parents. It has, in consequence, been
led to exclude religious instruction from the
process of education; has, indeed, abandoned
the work of education, and contented itself with
some sort of mental training which sharpens the
intellect but leaves the moral nature untouched
and unraised. As a result, the young lose reverence, lose the power of discerning what is high
and noble, and are only a more enlightened sort
of barbarians. Had the State confined itself to
encouraging and assisting the religious denomi-
nations to found and maintain schools, and to
giving aid to private educational enterprises, it
would have acted in harmony with our theory
of government, and we should be to-day a
worthier, more religious and not less enlightened people; while, from an economic point of
view, education would have been made vastly
cheaper. In the same way the tendency is now
to give the State control of public charities and
works of reform, whereas the proper method to
pursue is to have the State encourage and assist
denominational and private beneficence.

The recent labor agitations serve to show how

naturally our thoughts turn to State socialism whenever danger seems to threaten. If the State owned all railroads, it is asserted, troubles such as have disturbed the peace and prosperity of the country during the last few months would not occur. But in thus enlarging the functions of the government, we would double the number of its officials, and greatly increase the influence of professional politicians, who in various ways are doing more than all other classes combined to bring discredit upon democratic institutions. They are the men who praise the people and betray their interests, who flatter the working men and take the bribes of capitalists and wealthy corporations. They make possible the wholesale gambling, the stock-watering, the railway wrecking, the corruption of the judiciary and the legislature, which are in so many instances the agencies used in accumulating colossal fortunes. And the knowledge of this scandalous state of things, more than any other cause, favors the propagation of socialistic doctrines, and leads the people to hold the government in slight esteem, and to think there would be no great harm in taking from the money barons their ill-gotten goods. Thus the politicians are helping to undermine respect for law and belief in the sacredness of property. If there is no hope except in them, then there is no

hope at all. Politicians work through majorities, whereas minorities shape the higher destinies of nations; and it is all important that
we should learn that a man is not necessarily
visionary, or weak in mind, because he does not
run with the crowd. Gordon writes, in his
" Memoirs," that the British Empire has been
built up by adventurers, and not by the government. The principle involved in this fact
lies at the root of our social faith. The blood
which courses in our veins impels us to put our
trust in God and in our single might; and hence
the normal tendency of our institutions is to
increase the worth and influence of the individual, and to narrow the sphere and action of
government. If we lose confidence in ourselves,
and in every emergency look to the government
for help, how shall we escape the slavish mind
and coward heart?

The greatest peril to be feared from labor
organization is that the working men will be
led to put overmuch trust in these mechanical
contrivances, and will cease to look to the vital
sources of strength. When they have learned
to confide their dearest interests to a trades-
union, it will not be difficult to persuade them
to surrender themselves, body and soul, to a
socialistic State. Good government may secure
freedom and opportunity, but the effort, sobri-

ety, and intelligence of the individual can alone give worth and dignity to human life. Let political economists still insist upon their iron laws of wages, of supply and demand, but let us not lose our faith in free-will; for so long as we believe that there is an element of freedom in the individual, we shall feel that social evolution is not wholly fatal; and if much depends upon inexorable laws, much also depends upon the faith, hope, love, knowledge, pity, and courage of man. Sympathy, the spirit of humanity, the Godward mind, have wrought the miracles which political economy cannot even explain. Having done much, not for ourselves alone but for all nations, let us keep a brave heart, and believe that where all men think and act, the common sense of most will prevail, and wisdom, virtue, and nobler manhood be the result. It is a religious duty to work for the good of this country, and it is not easy to imagine that any one can love God or man and hate America.

IV.

CHARITY AND JUSTICE.

THE love of self is the radical passion of human nature. It is the love of life and of that which constitutes the good of life, and it is strongest in those who are most alive, in whom the vital current is deepest and mightiest. It is the inner source of strength in high and heroic souls, whether they seek to utter themselves in word or in deed, whether they strive for fame or for power or for union with God, through faith and devotion to truth and righteousness. Whatever the aim and the means, the end all men propose and follow is their own happiness, a more intense and enduring sense of their own life. Personality is enrooted in the love of self, and the higher the person the more completely does he identify himself with all that is other than himself. Savages, in their feeble attempts to think, consider things to be self-existent, each standing apart and independent, and hence the love of self is in them a selfish love. As they are incapable of perceiving that their relations to nature and to society are essential elements of their being, they imagine that the good of life for each one is separable from the general welfare. Hence they easily become false, cruel, treacherous, and revengeful. They lack humanity; they are the victims of instinct and impulse. They have the kind of social sense which is found in gregarious animals, but they are unable to ascend to the conception of the universal law which binds the whole race into a brotherhood. The degree in which individuals and societies rise above this separateness of childish and savage thought is a measure of the degree of their progress in religion and civilization. All advance is an ascent from the primitive and superficial self toward the true self, which is born of the union of the soul with truth, justice, and love. It is a process of self-estrangement, of self-denial, of self-abandonment. They alone enter the land of promise who quit the low and narrow house of their early thoughts and desires, and struggle with ceaseless effort and patience to reach the kingdom that is founded on the eternal principles of righteousness. They believe and know that peace, joy, and blessedness, which are the end to which the love of self points, can be attained only by those who seek and find the good of life in the service of the Father who is in heaven,

and of His children who are on earth. Self-
seeking is transformed into self-devotion; a
little world of petty cares and sordid interests is
abandoned, and the enduring world wherein
alone souls are at home opens wide its portals
to receive us. In isolation, the individual is
never great or impressive. To be so he must
identify himself with truth and justice, with
beauty and love. He must feel that he lives and
battles in the company of God and in that of the
noble and good, in some cause which is not
merely his own, but that of mankind.

He could never become man at all were it
not for the society and help of his fellows. The
human child would perish at once were it not
received, at birth, into the arms of intelligence
and love; and its prolonged infancy would issue
in nothing higher than savagery, were it not
fostered by beings in whom instinct has been
superseded by reflection and the sense of responsibility. In Christendom the individual enters
the world as the heir of all time. For him the
race has suffered and groped and toiled through
ages that have sunk into oblivion. For him
countless generations have fashioned language
— the social organ — into an instrument fitted
to express all that he can feel or know. The
clothes he wears, the home that shelters him
and makes him self-respecting, every implement

he uses, every contrivance that ministers to his comfort and security have been fashioned in the process of unnumbered centuries, by the pains and privations, by the sufferings and deaths, of tribes and peor'es to whose labors he gives no heed.

If he is born into a world where religion, science and morality, law, order and liberty, make it possible that he should lead a life of reverence, wisdom, and purity, and have rights and possessions which are defended by public opinion and the power of the combined strength of all; where his home is sacred, where his conscience is respected, where opportunity for the exercise of every talent is given, he owes all this not in any way at all to himself, but to others. And if in the midst of this world he himself is to have worth and significance, joy and peace, he must turn from himself and seek a better self through devotion to his fellow-men, whether they be in his home or in his church or in his nation or anywhere on God's round earth. He can have no real importance unless he ally himself with truth and justice and love, the knowledge and practice of which are within his reach because he is a member of a social organism. He is not self-made, he is a product of all the forces which have been at work in the universe from the beginning. He partakes of what nature provides, and he gathers the fruits of the seeds that saints and sages and heroes have sown up and down the world from immemorial ages. He is made strong and enduring by the struggles and labors of the race to which he belongs.

For him the martyrs have died, for him the poets have sung, for him the patient, tireless investigators have revealed the secrets which have given to the mind control of the forces that lie in the heavens, and in the earth. Mankind has lived for him; it is his duty to live for whomsoever he can help. His proper home is above nature: in the domain of reason, in the realm of freedom, in the kingdom of righteousness, in the spiritual world; where that which we communicate becomes doubly our own, where knowledge begets knowledge, where love kindles love, where charity burns the more, the more it becomes self-diffusive. A man cannot be wise or good or strong for himself alone. He is formed and confirmed by the virtues he imparts even more than by those he receives. If his heart be set on material things, he may gather them for himself, may grow hard and exclusive, ignoble and base; but if his supreme desire be for the things of the soul, he must communicate the blessings he gains, or they will vanish. In the home, in the church, in the

nation, the important thing for each one is
the help he gives, the benefits he bestows. He
who is not a source of faith, of courage, of
joy for those about him, has no well-spring
of divine life within himself. He must educate
if he would be educated; he must ennoble if
he would be made noble; he must diffuse religious thought and love if he would become
religious.

Every worthy form of individual activity is
altruistic. The money paid is never the equivalent of the work done; and whether the laborer
be farmer or builder, physician or teacher, he
must look beyond the price he gets to the good
he does; he must interfuse good-will and the
desire to be of help with all he does and with
all he receives for what he does, or he will
shrivel into something that appears to be alive,
but is dead. It must be his object to realize himself, not chiefly in his primitive physical self
with its material needs and sordid interests, but
he must bend all his energies to rise from the
low bed whereon nature has laid him to the
sphere where God manifests himself as Truth
and Love, as Beauty and Righteousness, as Life
Everlasting. Then he shall find himself in accord with the things that are permanent, with
the good that is absolute; then shall he learn
sympathy with all who live and are hard pressed

and beset with doubts and temptations, who are overburdened, whose feet are caught in the meshes of sin, whose hands hang helpless because joy in work is denied them.

Then shall he forget altruism and awaken to love — to the love that poised the heavens and holds the stars in place; that speaks to us when we look on flowers and ripening harvests and the faces of the fair and innocent; when we think of home and country and the graves of the dear ones who have fallen asleep — to the love which drew the Eternal Father from the infinite unseen to clothe himself with flesh, to walk with His children, to die for them, that henceforth every soul might understand that Love is the absolute fact behind, above, and beyond all that appears; that it is the charity of God; yea, God himself. What is a way of believing and thinking may be made also a way of feeling and acting. A passionate devotion to the salvation and welfare of men is aroused in innumerable souls, who, smitten with a sacred enthusiasm, leave father and mother and home and country that they may become the servants of the outcast, the abandoned, the fallen, of all whom inevitable circumstance and pitiless law overwhelm and crush.

To this new mood and temper no condition, no state in which a human being may be placed,

appears to be hopeless. The saving power of
infinite love is infinite. When reason despairs,
the heart still believes and hopes; and the best
and the noblest are not those who calculate, but
those who with divine confidence yield to the
impulses which descend from worlds to which
the understanding cannot rise. This is the
power which moves and consecrates the lives of
mothers and of all true lovers, of patriots and
saints, of virgins and martyrs. Life is not a
balance sheet — it is a breathing of God, awakening souls to service and to love. When a man
is prepared to live and to die for some good
cause that is all the world's, and not alone his
own, he has become a dweller in realms which
lie beyond the reach of the mere intellect. To
these heights the life and teaching of Christ
have lifted innumerable souls, enabling them to
love and serve not merely the beautiful, the
brave, and the generous, but to love and serve
those who have nothing amiable in themselves,
who are stricken with poverty, vice, and disease,
who distrust and hate us, who are our enemies
and their own. His coming is like the coming of
spring. The snows melt, the icy bands break,
the waters leap and sing, the earth awakens
from its death-like lethargy and clothes itself
in many-tinted vesture, the young are joyful,
and the old grow young again. So in the hu-

man world of faith and hope, of thought and
conduct, of love and service, Christ unseals the
fountains of sympathy and helpfulness and
mercy which lie in the heart of man, but which
cruelty and greed and tyranny had congealed.
In the ancient world, patriotism, which was its
special virtue, consecrated the instinct of hatred
for the foreigner. The earth was divided
among savages, barbarians, and civilized men
whose moral code was founded on a philosophy
of selfishness. Man's divine origin and destiny
were forgotten, the sacred meaning and worth
of life were ignored. The gods were not believed to take interest in human morality or
human welfare, and for the best of men there
was no refuge from the ruin wrought by greed
and lust and tyranny, save in a kind of stoic
indifference and despair. The virtues of mild-
·ness, mercy, serviceableness, chastity, and lowly-
mindedness were considered weaknesses and
defects. When Christ embodied in His deeds
and words the vital truth that God is a Father
who verily loves His children; that He is all-
holy; that righteousness is life; that only the
pure in heart can know Him; that those who
hunger and thirst to do His will enter His
kingdom, which is open to the meanest and most
abandoned, if they but repent and have faith
and charity, there was a revelation from heaven,

the opening of a fountain of immortal life in time and in eternity.

Enthusiasm, devotion, and love have no real object, no meaning, no worth, if man's life is but an apparition, an exhalation from a charnel house, a pathological growth, a mere dream of life in a universe essentially and eternally dead. One who believes not in God must cherish a thousand lies to save himself from despair. How can he who beneath the universal appearance that lures him sees but the deception, the trickery, the vileness, the vanity, which it veils, have a great mind or a loving heart? But this is what he must see if in all and above all he sees not God. Now, in Christ, the Eternal Father is made visible, and henceforth all may know that He is and that He is Love. The more we love one another the more plainly is this truth revealed to us. Love is the vital element of holiness, the spring and secret of righteousness, and there is no blessedness except in living and serving in the spirit of Christ.

Whatever change time may have wrought in opinions and in social conditions; whatever progress may have been made in scientific knowledge; whatever new machinery, whatever hitherto unutilized forces may have been placed at the disposition of man, it is still and must forever be true that nothing but the spirit of

Christian love can give us the power rightly to cheer, console, strengthen, guide, uplift, illumine, and purify one another. The money man spends on his lusts and vices might abolish poverty and fill the world with beauty, but not unless it were administered by hands of intelligence and love. None of the many schemes to overcome the misery and degradation which spring from vice, crime, and pauperism can attain the end without the ceaseless aid of right-loving men and women. Love not only bears all things, hopes all things; but it rejoices with the truth, and is quick to discover how help may be given.

Let the lovers of God and of man stand forth, and let the first word we speak to them affirm that without knowledge and science and wisdom and skill they can do little, are more apt, with all their zeal and fervor, to do harm than good. They do not love truly who neglect any means whatever whereby they may make themselves more able to be of service. It is easy to give money, but love cannot be bought, and the giving of money is not sufficient proof of love. Men spend lavishly to gratify the animal passions, which are the destroyers of love.   ..

They alone love who take a personal interest in those whom they would benefit, who reinforce their failing lives, not with bread

alone, but with sympathy and affection, with
faith and courage, with joy and gladness. We
feed domestic animals, but we are useless servants if we do nothing more than feed God's
poor who are our brethren. We must put ourselves in their place. Like students, we must
acquaint ourselves with their origins and environments; like friends, we must enter into
their failures and sorrows; like true men and
women, we must consider that whatever afflicts
them concerns us also. Love overcomes all,
subdues all things to its own divine purposes.;
It makes use of the sciences and the arts, of institutions and mechanical contrivances, to prevent or cure disease, to mitigate suffering, to
make the air and the earth wholesome, to con-
struct and build, to irrigate and drain, to improve in all possible ways the conditions and
environments of human life. We may not be
able, like the apostles and early disciples, to
work miracles, but centuries of Christian
thought and endeavor have, as the Saviour
foretold, given us the power to perform even
greater wonders. Knowledge has increased the
efficacy of faith; science has widened the boun-
daries of the empire of love. The change which
has taken place in our attitude toward the criminal is but an instance of a general transformation of opinion with regard to all who are

bound by the chains of ignorance, vice, and poverty.

We do not, like the savage and the barbarian, deal with the violators of law in the spirit of retaliation and vindictiveness; nor do we think it enough to immure them and render them harmless, but we hold it to be our duty to reform them; and above all, so far as this may be possible, we consider it a sacred obligation to do away with the causes which breed crime and misery. To do good to enemies is now recognized to be the duty of society not less than that of individuals. We have come to understand that the real criminal is often the social body itself rather than the man or woman it corrupts and then punishes. Here is an ascent into the world of reason, mercy, and righteousness, an unfolding of the divine purpose as made known by the Saviour, who revealed the sovereign nature of truth and love. His influence, more than all other causes, has lifted the multitude to a higher plane, where the spirit of sympathy and helpfulness breathes unhindered. We hold at least in theory, however we may fall in practice, that mankind are a family, that both the Church and the State are a home where all should be cherished, that the greater the weakness and misfortune the greater should be the care. We have abolished legalized slav-

6

ery, and the better among us are urged as by a divine voice to think no sacrifice too great whereby the condition of multitudes of toilers may be made more tolerable, more hopeful. We recognize that the rights of man are the rights of woman also, and slowly we are gaining insight into the truth that whatever is wrong for her is wrong for him. As it is our duty to protect children because they are weak and helpless, it is our duty to protect all who are weak and helpless. The young are by nature incapable of caring for themselves, and therefore the home, the Church and the State accept the responsibility of providing them with nourishment and nurture. The adult man and woman should not be weak or ignorant or vicious, and we feel that it is not their own fault chiefly, but the fault of the home, the Church and the State if they are so. We would therefore make helplessness, ignorance, and vice impossible. Religion inspires love, confidence, and courage, and science lights up the way of life with the torch of knowledge. As disease is largely preventable, we believe that vice, pauperism, and crime are also preventable. The law of causation is universal, and the cause being known, the finding of a remedy ought to lie within the reach of intelligence and love. Our progress consists largely in the discovery of remedies for igno-

rance and impotence. Quinine, drainage, and
sanitation have made vast regions habitable,
where hitherto healthful life had been impossible. The discovery of the causes of many of
the worst diseases has shown us how they may
readily be prevented or cured. The knowledge
of the causes of evil, whether physical or moral,
necessarily leads to the inquiry how they may
be suppressed or controlled. The cosmical and
geographical conditions which interfere with
the normal development of human endowments
we can hardly hope greatly to modify. In the
tropics the race is and probably will always be
indolent, ignorant, weak, and sensual. Heredity, too, plays a great part in the destiny of each
one. We are in mind, as in body, largely what
we have assimilated or what heredity—which is
the outcome of endless assimilations—makes us.
Those who are born with a taint in the blood,
with perverted instincts and enfeebled wills,
not only fall into vice more easily than others,
but they are also more difficult to reclaim. If
man shall ever learn to do for his own kind
what breeding and training enable him to do
for various strains of domestic animals, he will
have discovered an effective means for prevent-
ing crime and misery. But what he calls his
rights, which often are but his prejudices and
passions, will probably continue to keep him

from treating his own species with the wisdom with which he manages inferior creatures. Reckless and senseless marriages are an inexhaustible source of evil. Many of our people enter into wedlock as thoughtlessly as they take a stroll or fall asleep, and the result is quarrels, contentions, divorces, and children reared in an atmosphere which blights their tender lives. Hence crime among the young is increasing far more rapidly than the population grows. So long as this poison fountain remains open, so long will vice and pauperism continue to breed degradation and wretchedness. Homes that are hells thwart the wisest efforts to reform abuses. They hinder the school, weaken the church, and undermine the social fabric. Our chaotic and lax marriage laws encourage and facilitate imprudent marriages, but the origin of the evil lies deeper. Institutions, it has been said, are in the control of men; public opinion in that of women. Women decide how we shall build and furnish our houses, what we shall eat and wear, what we shall find beautiful and entertaining, where we shall live, what we shall read, whom we shall consider friend or foe, what beliefs or prejudices we shall hold, what religion we shall have. From them we learn our mother tongue, from them our notions of right and wrong, of propriety and justice. If they were more large-minded, more intelligent, more unselfish, more serious, more loving, three-fourths of the depravity and sin which make life a curse would disappear. The fountain-head of social good or evil, of vice and crime, or of honor and virtue is in the home; and the wife and the mother make or unmake the home. Whatever view we may take as to whether man or woman was the more guilty primal offender, woman bears the greater responsibility for the wrongs and miseries which afflict and oppress the modern world, since the force of public opinion, which is in her keeping, is mightier than riches and armies and laws. More than any age since the beginning of time we have given opportunity to woman, have placed her in the seat of influence and power; and shall she prove false, or frail, or ungrateful, traitorous to the vast confidence which all that is noblest and most chivalrous in man has led him to repose in her?

Doubtless her increasing dominion has helped to arouse in our public life greater sympathy and tenderness, a more complete revulsion from cruelty, whether to man or beast. But more than pity we need justice, which is the first and greatest charity. The most grievous injustice which oppresses us, of which the weak and the poor, the laborers and their wives and children, are the chief victims, has its source in the political corruption which taints our whole public life, and more especially the conduct of our municipal affairs. It not only stamps upon our name a brand of infamy in the eyes of foreign nations; it disheartens the best among us, and makes reform seem impossible. It not only impoverishes, but it disheartens and dechristianizes the laboring populations of our cities. It is the foe of civilization, of religion, of morality; of God and of man. It thrives in the mephitic air of saloons and brothels and gambling hells. It makes the rich its accomplices and compels the respectable to connive at its iniquities and infamies. It perverts the public conscience, it destroys the sense of responsibility, it renders efforts at reform abortive. In the presence of this moral plague even the wisest and the bravest are bewildered and discouraged. No subject is more worthy of the attention of those who are interested in the improvement of social life and conditions. Legislation can accomplish little unless it be supported by a more humàne, a more enlightened, a more Christian public opinion. Here again, therefore, we need the assistance of noble-minded and educated women. If in the home, in the school, and in the church, where woman's influence is potent, if not paramount, the sentiment that corrupt politicians are more criminal than convicts, be awakened and fostered, good will have been done. Were it possible that the daily press should take a sincere and serious interest in whatever concerns the public morals, what a beneficent power it might exert! But this cannot be hoped for while the newspaper continues to be chiefly a commercial enterprise; for when the primary consideration is pecuniary profit, it will be deemed proper to publish whatever may excite curiosity, even though it pander to morbid cravings and prurient propensities. In the actual conditions, the machinery and institutions created to deal with the violators of the laws are, in a large measure, the agencies whereby vice and crime are produced and diffused. The delinquents who are incarcerated are chiefly the poor, who had they money to pay the fines would escape imprisonment. The heaviest punishment is inflicted on the most helpless, and frequently on the least guilty; and thus the morally weak, the victims of unfortunate environments, are degraded, hardened, and made habitual offenders. Nearly one-half of the several millions annually arrested become chronic criminals. In the face of the theory that punishment should be reformatory and preventive, the fact remains that in our hands it is still largely a cause of corruption and of the spread of vice. Our city prisons and station houses are often nurseries of crime, and this may be affirmed also of many of our county jails and poorhouses. A recognized authority on this subject has said that if there is an iniquity in the land to-day it is the county jail system; that there is no greater iniquity in the world than the jail system of the United States. But the discussion of this and analogous questions would carry us beyond our present aim. It is enough to have called attention to the fact that it is the part of wisdom to refuse to yield unreservedly to our American spirit of optimism. All past ages when compared with our own were, in a sense, ages of ignorance, and there may be reasons for thinking that the man of the future will place our century in the same category. A dark age certainly it shall be called when considered from the point of view of conduct, when character is held to be the only sufficient test of enlightenment. The immature and the degenerate prefer pleasure to virtue and power, and those who prefer money to truth and love are also immature or degenerate. Greed, not less than sensuality, marks epochs in which all things are verging toward ruin. We are at present under the tyrannous sway of the spirit of commercialism and expansion, and our very thought is made subservient to the ideal of vulgar success; but those who have best insight have a fine scorn of current opinion. They are able to do without its approval, and they end by receiving it.

Emerson says that America is God's great charity to the race; but true religion working with the added power which science gives is greater than America: it will purify, ennoble, and transform our life into some likeness to the divine ideals, which as yet we but vaguely discern. We have already learned that a man's chief value does not lie in his ability to conquer with sword and shell, and we are coming to understand that it lies just as little in his ability to manipulate machinery or to get money.

Comte thinks that Christianity is the consecration of egoism; and it is a fact that it regards primarily the individual and asserts the supreme worth of personality. But it also insists that the individual can rightly develop and find himself only in devoting his thought and life to the love and service of God and his fellow-man. It would found on earth a kingdom of heaven in which obedience to the will of the Eternal Father (which is good-will to man) shall be an all-controlling constitutional principle and law; and beneficence the universal means of personal and social advancement. We must be benefactors that we may become able to love our fellows, for if we incline to hate those whom we wrong, more surely are we drawn to love those to whom we do good.

They who live with whatsoever things are true, just, gracious, pure, and amiable, continue to grow in mental and moral power; and the good of life lies in the mental and moral dispositions which a spiritual faith and disinterested conduct create and foster within us. As matter is but life's setting, not its substance, so if we would go to the succor of those who fail in right living we must give them our interest, sympathy, confidence, and affection more than our money. The special vice of the thriftless and delinquent is heedlessness and recklessness. We must train them to forethought, attention, and consideration; and personal influence, not almsgiving, is the proper means whereby this may be accomplished. If we would save them, we must save them from themselves. The purest charity consists in doing the spiritual rather than in doing the corporal works of mercy, since the essential good is the good of the soul. Let us have confidence in whatever increases the power of the soul; confidence therefore in the virtues of religion, which are faith, hope, and love; confidence in knowledge, science, freedom, and labor, persuaded that riches are good only when they are the possessions of the wise and good.

It is easier to be generous than to be just. The generous win approval, while the just are often misunderstood and suspected of lack of heart. The poor love the poor because they give their thought and time to one another. They do not love the rich because the rich give them only money. Mere advice has little efficacy, for what we all need in nearly all situations is not so much a clearer view of right, as a more fervent desire, a more determined will to do right; and advice cannot supply this. No system of dogma or morals, however much it be preached, can regenerate the world. If men are to be converted and transformed, they must be brought close to Christ himself, must learn to know and love Him, as St. John and St. Luke, St. Francis and St. Vincent de Paul knew and loved Him; they must be brought to believe and feel that as He is one with the Father, so are we all verily God's children. If reason alone controlled us the world would be a waste. If the universe of metaphysics and of science were not an abstraction, it would be a hell where faith, hope, and love would become impossible; for these are nourished and kept alive, not by speculation and research, but by unselfish service, generous deeds, and heroic endeavor.

Among the ancients the unfortunate were held to be accursed, hateful to the divinities, and consequently without title to the pity of men. In nothing has Christ wrought a more radical change than in the world's attitude toward the weak and heavy laden. He withstood the super-. stition and mercilessness to which centuries had given a kind of religious sanction, and taught by word and deed that the more sinful, the more ignorant, the more abandoned our fellows are, the greater their claim on our attention and service. His life and doctrines have produced a mighty and beneficent revolution in their be- half; and yet much of the old hardness and injustice still survives both in society and in innumerable individuals who call themselves followers of the all-loving and all-helpful Saviour. What multitudes there are who pass by and ignore the misery and suffering they cannot but see, who despise the poverty- stricken, who are hard and bitter toward the erring; how many who imagine they serve God by hating and maligning one another; who are hindrances to the spread of the kingdom for whose coming they pray! As when we look in a mirror we try to see ourselves in a favorable light, so when by introspection we attempt to get a glimpse of our inner being, we instinctively take the points of view which best reveal our qualities and hide our defects. If we should strive honestly to see ourselves as we are, self-complacency would quickly die within us.

If we were true Christians we should be able to labor for our fellows with such confidence and enthusiasm that nor baseness, nor ingratitude, nor faithlessness, nor apostasy from light and love of however many of those we seek to help would have power to cool our ardor or diminish our zeal. Though the world about us should appear to crave for nothing but money and sensation, we would none the less dedicate whatever of ability God has given us to redeem our brothers from themselves; and if in the end we should have accomplished nothing, we should at least have escaped an ignoble life.

The purest pleasure is to give pleasure, and the highest glory belongs to those who labor earnestly, both by thinking and by doing, to make truth, justice, and love prevail. The universe was made for every one of us, and for each one the world will be fair and pleasant in the degree in which he strives to make it so for others. It is not possible to respect one's self and to make no sacrifice for one's fellowmen. In coming closer to one another to help those who need help, we shall make ourselves more capable of seeing and confessing the truth which the life and work and words of Christ reveal.

What is true of us as individual men and
women applies with equal force to our national
life. The ends to which as a people we are called
to devote ourselves are religion, education, justice, and charity. If we fail in this, wealth and
numbers and the conquest of distant lands will
have no power to save us from ruin and shame.
Nothing but a civilization resting on a basis of
righteousness and morality can make popular
government permanent. If we are to look, not
to the triumphs of the moment, but to lasting
results for which the whole world shall be grateful, we must trust to the largest thought and the
purest love; for so surely as God is, so surely
are they destined to prevail. Tyranny is the foe
of liberty; greed, of justice; brute force, of
mercy and goodness; and wars, which spring
from the barbarous passion for conquest, from
covetousness, from the savage's delight in victory won by cunning and physical strength,
pervert judgment, destroy right feeling, and
foster the vices which weaken, harden, and blind
the people, and lead the way to destruction.
Unless we remain sensitive to moral distinctions,
unless we prefer justice and mercy to dominion
over the kingdoms of the earth, we shall enter
the open ways along which the republics and
empires of the past have rushed to shame and
destruction. If, then, we love America; if we

believe in the brotherhood of mankind, in equal opportunity and freedom for all of God's children, let us turn from dehumanizing greed, from vainglory and pride, to follow after truth and justice and love.

V.

WOMAN AND THE CHRISTIAN RELIGION.

NO man can write worthily of woman who does not approach his subject with a kind of religious reverence; and a true man will ever treat woman, both in life and in literature, not with justice merely, but with generous sympathy. Into her arms we are born, on her breast our helpless cries are hushed, and her hands close our eyes when the light is gone. Watching her lips, our own become vocal; in her eyes we read the mystery of faith, hope, and love; led by her hand, we learn to look up and to walk in the way of obedience to law. We owe to her, as mother, as sister, as wife, as friend, the tenderest emotions of life, the purest aspirations of the soul, the noblest elements of character, and the completest sympathy in all our joy and sorrow. She weaves flowers of heaven into the vesture of earthly life. In poetry, painting, sculpture, and religion, she gives us ideals of the fair and beautiful. Innocence is a woman, chastity is a woman, charity is a woman. And yet, true as all this is and is felt to be throughout Christendom, such views and sentiments, when considered in the light of history, séem to be little less than absurd. The poets have sung divinely of woman, but man has treated her inhumanly. At the origin of society she is everywhere a drudge, a slave, a chattel. Among the Babylonians, we know from Herodotus, it was the custom to offer women for sale to the highest bidder, and every woman was required, at least for a time, to put a price on her virtue. With the Lydians this was a universal practice. The Syrians, to the immolation of children to idols, joined the compulsory sacrifice of woman's honor. Strabo affirms that even the most distinguished families among the Armenians presented their daughters to the goddess of debauch in the temple of Anaïtis; and the same writer tells us that a law of the Medes required every man to have not less than seven wives. That polygamy and infanticide were common among the Persians is a fact to which Herodotus testifies, who also says that the Scythians were promiscuous in their relations with women, were conjugal despots, and immolated widows on the graves of their husbands. And Strabo asserts that the ancient Hindoos bought their wives, treated them as slaves, and burned them when their husbands died. Among the Mongols, community of women was consecrated both by law and custom. In Egypt, Diodorus tells us, unlimited polygamy was lawful to all except the priests; and the support of the family, by the rudest labors, and often by the sale of virtue, devolved upon woman, while the men stayed at home to nurse and knit. In Greece woman held a less degraded position. She was not the slave of her husband, but, with the exception of a certain class of public women, she was reared in ignorance and confined to the nursing of children and to domestic drudgery. When her husband entertained his friends, she was not permitted to sit at table. The Grecian view of marriage is physico-political. Even in the heroic epoch of Homer, there is no trace of the sentiment of love as it is known to us. Of the many suitors of Penelope, not one seeks to render himself worthy of her love. The famous passage in which Homer describes the parting of Hector from Andromache, depicts the great hero's concern for his son, rather than for his wife; and Andromache is embraced by Pyrrhus, the son of the slayer of her husband. Menelaus takes Helen back in complete indifference, after she had lived ten years with Paris. Telemachus rudely tells his mother to go back to her spinning-wheel, and that to speak among men belongs only to man. The husband bought his wife, and the woman taken captive was reduced to slavery and sold as a chattel. Woman's work in the Homeric period was to draw water, to wash, to grind corn, to make the fire, and to perform all the most menial and even indecent labors for men. Hesiod, who probably belongs to this period, calls women " an accursed brood, and the chief scourge of the human race." And Æschylus, at a later date, declares that woman is the direst scourge both of the State and the home. The daily prayer of Socrates was a thanksgiving to the gods that he had been born neither a slave nor a woman; and Aristotle teaches that woman is by nature the inferior of man. Plato, in his " Republic," takes a purely political view of woman, and would have the propagation of the human race made subject to the principles that guide stock-raisers in the breeding of animals. In the historical age of Greece, a slight improvement in the legal position of woman was accompanied by her social degradation. Virtuous women were kept in ignorance and seclusion, and the place of honor was given to courtesans. The companionship of Socrates and Theodota, and Plato's presence in the house of Aspasia, without even the remotest suspicion that such a state of affairs was reprehensible, make it unnecessary to use other arguments to show the ineffable degradation to which woman had been brought in the most brilliant epoch of Grecian civilization.

In the earliest days the Romans bought or captured their wives; and women were not permitted to own or inherit property. Romulus gave the husband absolute authority over the wife, even to the right of life and death. Egnacius Menecius was scarcely blamed for killing his wife, though she had been guilty of nothing more grievous than merely tasting wine. " Slacken the rein," said Cato, speaking of woman, "and you will afterwards strive in vain to check the mad career of that unreasoning animal." The Romans habitually contrasted the majesty of man (*majestas virorum*) with the imbecility, frivolity, and weakness of woman (*sexus imbecillis, levis, impar laboribus*). As they drowned weak and deformed children, so they treated woman as an inferior and a slave. In Rome, as in Greece, as the laws were made more just to woman, her moral and social degradation was intensified. There is nothing sadder in human history than the condition of women during the decline of the Roman State. A depravity of which it is impossible to speak without becoming indelicate grew like a leprosy into the lives of women of every class, until, as Plutarch says, they seemed to have been born only for luxury and sensuality. Asiatic slaves of surpassing beauty were introduced into every patrician house, and Roman matrons, throwing aside even the appearance of decency, delivered themselves up to the most revolting vice. Seneca says, "They vied with men in licentiousness." There was a universal aversion to marriage, and a weariness of life itself. The Roman Empire had become a slough of blood and filth.

If we turn to the barbarous populations from which the modern Christian nations have been developed, we find no marked change for the better in the condition of woman. Certain authors, in their zeal to deny all beneficent influence to the Christian religion, have sought to make it appear that the present position of women in the civilized world is, in a great measure, to be ascribed to the reverence in which it is supposed woman was held by the Teutonic tribes that on the downfall of the Roman Empire gained control of a large part of Europe. They form this opinion upon information derived from Tacitus, who, in his account of the manners and customs of the Germans, says:

" They think there is in women something holy and prophetical; they do not despise their counsels, and they listen to their predictions. In the time of the divine Vespasian we have seen the greater part of them regard Velleda as a goddess."

But Tacitus here alludes manifestly to a superstitious belief in woman as a sorceress and prophetess, and any conclusions that we may attempt to draw from his words as to woman's social position among these barbarous tribes must be valueless. Similar beliefs and analogous customs, as Guizot has remarked, have existed among many savage and barbarous peoples. Tacitus, indeed, expressly says in another passage, that the authority of Velleda was due to a superstition among the Germans that led them to look upon many women as prophetesses; and the witchcraft of the middle ages, and even that of New England, at a later day, for which Christianity has been held accountable, was the survival of an ancient pagan superstition, which it required centuries to erase from the popular imagination. It must be borne in mind, too, that Tacitus had never crossed the Rhine, and that his knowledge of the social customs of the barbarians was derived from others, whose accounts may or may not have been trustworthy. Again, Tacitus wrote in the mephitic air of Roman corruption, and the indignation with which the moral degradation of his countrymen filled him must have led him to

paint in brighter colors the life of barbarians
who could not have been so depraved as the
civilized men whom he knew. We know, at all
events, that the lot of woman among the Teutonic tribes was what it has always been among
barbarous peoples. The slayer of a woman capable of bearing children was made to pay a fine
of about six dollars; if she was too young or
too old to become a mother, the fine was put at
two dollars. It is the old Greek view, in which
woman is valuable because without her it is not
possible to have man. The husband bought his
wife, and if she became unfaithful he drove
her with rods through the village in a state of
nudity. The sentiment of modesty and holy
shame, which is so essential a part of Christian
reverence for woman, could hardly have existed
among these populations, since we know from
Tacitus that custom permitted the men and
women to bathe promiscuously. Polygamy was
conceded in principle, since kings and nobles
were permitted to have several wives. " A
slave," says Strabo, " woman was compelled to
toil for her husband during his life, and at his
death she was immolated on his grave, that she
might continue to serve him in another world."
Among the other barbarous peoples of Europe,
woman's lot was still more deplorable. Cæsar's
account of the tribes that inhabited England

gives us an insight into a state of depravity to which history can hardly furnish a parallel.

It is not difficult to account for this world-wide inhumanity of man to woman. Throughout all pre-Christian history the law of superior strength was the rule of conduct. The strongest governed, and governed in virtue of their strength, and not in virtue of any moral sanction or divine authority.

This is at all times true of savage and barbarous hordes; and it is, in a general way, true of the pagan States of Greece and Rome. The notion that man has duties to his fellow-man, even though he be wholly in his power, did not enter into the view of human life. Captives, therefore, might be put to death, or reduced to a state of slavery worse than death. The slave was a chattel; the master was free to treat him as he treated his ass or his dog. Among pagans, the later stoics were the first to teach that masters are bound by ties of moral obligation to their slaves, and how far these views may have been the result of Christian influences it is not easy to determine. When strength is made the measure of right, woman is inevitably driven to the wall. Nature, in making her a mother, makes her weak — takes a part of her blood, her mind, and her heart to give it to another. Child-bearing and child-rearing place her at a disadvantage. Were she even physically stronger and mentally more capable than man, the infirmities and the duties inseparable from her sex would make it impossible for her to cope with him in the life-struggle. Hence, wherever the law of strength has been accepted as the rule of life, man has treated woman as Petruchio proposed to treat Katherina:

> "I will be master of what is mine own,
>   She is my goods, my chattels; she is my house,
>   My household stuff, my field, my barn,
>   My horse, my ox, my ass, my anything."

The savage went wife hunting, as he went wolf or bear hunting, and brought the captive home to be his slave. The barbarian, too, captured his woman in war, or bought her. The civilized pagan was a polygamist, or at least looked upon himself as wholly free from all obligations of marital fidelity.

If this is, in general outlines, the history of woman except in Christendom, it is pertinent to ask whether the Christian religion bears any causal relation to her actual position in the civilized world. When Christ came, woman, like the slave, was everywhere without honor, without freedom, without hope. Men, bearing the curse of their own depravity, sank into the

depths of moral infamy to which they had reduced the poor and the weak. Surrounded by
human herds to whom vice in its most degrading forms had become a second nature, they
breathed an atmosphere of corruption, in which
the moral sense perished. Life grew to be a
kind of remittent fever alternating between lust
and blood. Here and there a stray voice pro-
tested, but only in tones of despair. The masses
of mankind — the slave and the woman — had
been reduced to a state so pitiable that possibly
nothing short of the coming of God himself, in
sorrow and in weakness, could have inspired
the courage even to dream of better things.
Hope had fled; the world was prostrate; in
the mephitic air of unnatural sensual indulgence the soul was stifled; woman had lost
even the attractiveness of sex, and a thousand
slaves could hardly feed the stomach of Dives.
To such a world Jesus Christ came, and took
Lazarus in His arms, and called upon all who
believed in God to follow Him in the service of
outraged humanity. Before any moral progress
could be hoped for, new ideas had to be grafted
in the human mind, ideas as to what man is in
himself, as to what is due to him in virtue of
his very nature; new doctrines concerning the
duties of all men to all men, and especially of
the strong to the weak, of the rich to the poor,

of man to woman. Christ sees the soul. The soul determines the value of human life, and the soul of the child, of the slave, of woman, is as sacred as the soul of Cæsar. " There is neither Jew nor Greek; there is neither bond nor free; there is neither male nor female. For you are all one in Christ Jesus." That which is supreme in Christ is love. He pours the boundless love of God into the channels in which human life flows. In His presence up-glows the purest, the strongest, the most un-quenchable love that exists or has existed on earth; and He turns this stream of divine charity into the desert of human wretchedness and woe, to refresh and gladden the hearts of the poor and the forlorn, of the slave and the beggar, and of woman, the great outcast of humanity. He sends those who love Him to feed the hungry, to give drink to the thirsty, to clothe the naked, to ransom the captive, to visit the sick. Wherever a human being suffers wrong or want, there is Christ to be loved and to be served. Homer is not so much the father of all our poetry, nor Socrates so much the master of all our intellectual discipline, as is Christ the fountain-head of the humanitarian love that makes men helpful to the weak and the wronged. In lifting the soul into the full light of God's presence, He not only gave a new measure of the value of life, but a new meaning to authority. The supremacy of force is supplanted by the supremacy of truth and justice, of love and mercy. Slaves and beggars will now appeal from emperors and senates to God, in the name of the soul, redeemed by Christ. Henceforth, to be man is to be God-like; to be an emperor is to be human. In the light of this truth, woman becomes the equal of man. Hence polygamy is abolished, and marriage is of one with one, and for life. Wedded love becomes sacramental love, and the tenderness with which Christ loves His Church becomes the symbol of the love of husband for wife. " He that loveth his wife," says St. Paul, " loveth himself. For no man ever hated his own flesh, but nourisheth and cherisheth it, as also Christ doth his Church." Thus the family becomes a lesser church, the home a sanctuary, and woman is God's providence, sitting by each man's hearth-fire. Eve withdraws, and the Virgin Mother is made the ideal woman. No Amazon here, no Spartan mother, no stern mother of the Gracchi, no goddess of sensual love, no fair slave of man's animal appetites; but woman, pure, gentle, tender, loving, patient, strong; the world's benefactress, because, through her, divine manhood lives on earth, and peace, love, mercy, and righteousness prevail. With this new ideal of womanhood, the exaltation of the beauty and moral worth of perfect chastity is intimately associated. The selfishness of man, which is chiefly shown in the indulgence of his sensual passions, is woman's most terrible enemy. Love is pure and gentle; lust is coarse and brutal. Love is born of the soul, and not of the senses; and when this celestial flower first blooms under the eyes of a pure youth and a fair maiden, they are lifted to infinite heights, and the sad side of love is the disenchantment that comes when they are awakened from their dream. Nothing tends more to exalt the passion of pure love than reverence for virginity, real belief in the sacredness of womanly virtue. Those only are worthy of the love of woman who, like King Arthur's knights, bind themselves —

> " To lead sweet lives in purest chastity,
> To love one maiden only, cleave to her,
> And worship her by years of noble deeds."

This exaltation of perfect chastity is the most emphatic assertion of the truth that woman does not exist simply for man; that the sphere of her activity is not bounded by the duties of wife and mother. She may love Jesus Christ, and, with no man for her husband, become a ministering angel of light and love to the wide world.

Purity, meekness, patience, faith, and love —
which are the virtues that our blessed Lord
most emphasizes — are, above all, womanly virtues. He does not exalt intellect, courage, and
strength, but gentleness, and lovingness, and
helpfulness. The Christian hero even, like all
heroines, shows his supreme strength in suffering rather than in doing. To the most wretched
phase even of woman's existence the Saviour
has brought the healing of His heavenly grace.
In all literature, sacred and profane, there is
nothing so touching, so tender and consoling,
as the Gospel episode of Magdalene; and he
who looks with more complacency upon Aspasia
with Plato at her feet than upon Magdalene at
the feet of Jesus is self-condemned. If we take
a view of Christian history in the light of the
ideals that Christ has given us, there is, of
course, disappointment. The ideal never becomes real in this earthly existence, and since
even the best reach not these heights, the multitude, of course, remain far below. Ideals are
like the mountain-peaks that gleam amid the
azure heavens; we look up to them with delight, but the ascent wearies, and when on the
summit we find the air too fine for our coarse
breathing, and in the solitude we miss the crowd
and grow lonely. Nevertheless, on these snow-
capped heights are born the spring showers and

the summer rains, which nourish the growing corn and the ripening grain. But if Christian society has not realized its ideals concerning woman, it has never been without their elevating and refining influence. To the action of the Church in the middle ages we are indebted for the monogamic family, which lies at the basis of our civilization and is the stronghold of all that is best in our social life. Had not popes and bishops withstood kings and barons when they sought to continue the polygamous practices that among the German barbarians were lawful, monogamy would have perished among the ruling classes of Europe; and with the development of popular power, had such development then been possible, woman would have fallen to the place that she to-day occupies in Mohammedan countries. Indeed, the preservation of all western Europe from the blight of Mohammedanism is due to the action of the Church, which united and was alone able to unite the warring factions of western semi-barbarians, and to hurl them, century after century, against the strongholds of the hordes whose dream of heaven was a place of sensual delights.

The objection has often been urged, that in making man the head of the family the Church is unjust to woman. But the family is an organic unity, and cannot exist without subordination and authority. Either the husband or the wife must be the depository of domestic authority, and unless it can be shown that woman is better fitted than man to exercise this power, no injustice has been done. Physically man is stronger than woman; he is better able to confront the world and to do the work by which the members of the family are maintained in health and comfort. Historically, society grows out of a warlike and barbarous state of life; and since women are less fitted for war than men, the defense of property and rights is naturally intrusted to those whose hands hold the sword. But it is not necessary to examine into the genesis and evolution of society to find reasons for giving the headship of the family to man; we need but look into the heart of woman to see there an impulse as strong as life to look up to and follow the man she loves. Between man and woman there ought to be no question of superiority or inferiority; they are unlike, and in nothing do they differ more than in their relative power to escape from their impressions. A woman understands only what she feels, whereas a man may grow to be able to look at things as they are in themselves, remaining the while indifferent to their relations to himself. Hence women are superior to men in those virtues in which the essential element is right feeling. They believe more, hope more, and love more than men. They are more compassionate, more capable of remaining faithful to those who are unworthy of their love, because they consider only the love they feel, and give comparatively little heed to its object. Men, on the other hand, are superior in the virtues that spring less from sentiment and depend rather on the nature of things, — their eternal fitness, —as justice, fortitude, equanimity, wisdom, prudence. This difference in character determines their position in domestic and social relations; nor would there be gain for either man or woman if they could be made less unlike. The charm, as well as the helpfulness, of their relations lies in their differences, and not in their likenesses. They are complementary; each needs the qualities of the other, and their wants are the bond of union. The opposition of men and women to so-called woman's rights comes, doubtless, in many instances from a belief that to throw woman into public life is to make her less womanly. Nor gods nor men love a mannish woman or a womanish man. The unfairness with which woman is treated in the legislation of the mediæval epoch may be traced to the barbarous ideas concerning woman that partially survived in Europe centuries after our

ancestors had been converted to Christianity;
nor has this injustice even yet disappeared from
the statute-books of the civilized nations. The
causes that have led to the improvement of.
woman's condition among the Christian nations
are, in general, the same that have developed
our civilization. Whatever influences have been
active in the abolition of slavery, in securing
popular rights, free government, protection for
children and the poor, in bringing knowledge
within the reach of all, and thereby spreading
abroad juster and more humane principles of
conduct, have also wrought for the welfare of
woman; and it is not necessary to point out how
intimately all this progress is associated with
the social action of the Christian religion. The
spirit of chivalry is the outgrowth of the Christian ideal of womanhood. To maintain that
Christianity crushed out " the feminine element,
and, more than all other influences combined,
plunged the world into the dark ages," is to
indulge in a kind of declamation that, for the
past half-century at least, has become impossible
to enlightened minds. To say that the doctrine
of original sin throws the guilt exclusively or
chiefly on woman, is merely to affirm one's ignorance of Christian teaching. St. Ambrose, one
of the four great doctors of the Western Church,
declares that woman's fault in the original fall

was less than that of man, as her bearing was beyond question more generous. And then the Catholic Church at least teaches that Mary has more than made good any wrong that Eve may have done. To assert that in the Christian religion " the godhead is a trinity of males " is to be at once ignorant and coarse. God is neither male nor female, as in Christ there is neither male nor female. To proclaim that the Christian religion teaches that " woman is an after-thought in creation, sex a crime, marriage a condition of slavery for woman and defilement for man, and maternity a curse," is to mistake rant for reason, declamation for argument. In fact, the advocates of woman's rights too often take this false and therefore offensive tone. They speak like people who have grievances; and to have a grievance is to be a bore. They scold; and when women scold, whether in public or in private, men may not be able to answer them, but they grow sullen and cease to be helpful. To be persuasive, woman must be amiable; and to be strong, she must speak from a loving heart, and not from a sour mind. Whoever is thoroughly imbued with the spirit of Christianity must sympathize with all movements having as their object the giving to woman the full possession of her rights. No law that is unjust to her should exist in Christendom. She should

·not be shut out from any career that offers to her the means of an honest livelihood. For the same work she should receive the same wages as a man, and should hold her property in virtue of the same right that secures to him the possession of his own. For wrong-doing of whatever kind she should not be made to suffer a severer punishment than is inflicted upon man. The world will continue to be unjust to her until public opinion makes the impure man as odious as it makes the impure woman.

The best interests of mankind, of the Church and the State, will be served by widening and strengthening woman's influence. The ancient civilization perished because woman was degraded, and ours will be perpetuated by a pure, believing, self-reverent, and enlightened womanhood. Woman here in the United States is more religious, more moral, and more intelligent than man; more intelligent in the sense of greater openness to ideas, greater flexibility of mind, and a wider acquaintance with literature; and whatever is really good for her must be good for our religion and civilization. She " stays all the fair young planet in her hands."

VI.

EMOTION AND TRUTH.

[Address delivered on the twenty-fifth anniversary of the
establishment of the diocese of Peoria.]

WHATEVER stirs emotion disturbs judgment. This most beautiful May time, a
great concourse of people, a throng of bishops
and priests in symbolic vesture; music, pleading
for power to utter the thought and love of the
Eternal, or bursting forth in swelling volumes
of sound that roll and rise, borne on viewless
wings, to the throne of God; rites and cere-
monies, hallowed by association with the divinest faith and the noblest memories, with the
heroic sufferings and triumphs of millions of
men and women — the fine flower and fruit of
humanity — who century after century for more
than fifty generations have taken their stand on
the world-wide battlefield, steadfast until swal-
lowed in the vortices of visible things, to re-live
in the ever-enduring universe of pure spirits —
all this exalts the imagination and lifts to
spheres where feeling is spontaneous and delib-
eration difficult.

For most of us who are gathered here the day itself brings recollections which for each one are tender and moving, as with varying shade and circumstance they twine around the founding of parishes, the building of churches and schools and homes of mercy and beneficence, that in more than a hundred towns and villages, and on wide prairies amid the growing corn and the ripening harvest, have risen at the call of faith and at the promptings of a generosity that seems to annul selfish impulse, so long as there is good to be done — recollections of youthful courage, high hope, and pertinacious labor undertaken for what each one believed to be most divine, and endured for the love of what is holiest. It is inevitable, therefore, that emotions swell within us, which dispose us to accept as truth words which sober reason is reluctant to approve. But best reason rests in Love, from which the universe has sprung, of whose deepest heart certainly our religion is born; and since from this same source the sentiments which inspire us to-day rise like a fountain's pure, light-seeking waters, why may we not believe and affirm that what such emotion has awakened and bodied forth in word and deed is very truth? Not indeed logical or scientific truth — a skeleton of formulas and facts — but the truth which is borne in upon the soul when mothers sing their children to sleep, when lovers sitting side by side watch the sun sinking beneath the horizon, and the stars as one by one they smile from infinitude on the homes of men; such truth as the flowers speak, when from their lowly beds they look up and laugh before us; such as children reveal and impersonate when heaven is mirrored in their pure eyes and innocent faces.

If truth were but the naked fact, where should there be found room for the ineffable charm which interfuses itself with the glow of dawn and sunset, with the light that falls from starlit skies and from the countenances of those we love; for the passion and patience, the trust and longing, the sacrifice and aspiration, which impel the soul to transcend the limitations of time and space and which give to human life its power and blessedness?

When we recall the years that are no more, the paths we trod in childhood, the concert of voices that in the long ago made the woodland ring with music, the quick current of youthful blood athrill with high hopes and noble resolves, and suddenly are made aware that it has all dissolved into emptiness and become as though it had never been, it is not possible to remain cold and impassive. When we turn to the beginning of our early manhood, as issuing with sublime self-confidence from the portals of

our Alma Mater, we vowed to walk and work
with Christ, to illumine, to guide, to strengthen,
to console, and to save men, and are made
deeply conscious how little our purposes have
fulfilled themselves in deeds, we are softened
and sobered, grow lowly-minded and meek,
like those who contemplate ruins which the
centuries have wrought. In such mood all
vanity and self-complacency die within us, and
words of praise and commendation sound like
mockery.

The achievements of even the genuinely
great, if they be considered in the light of the
Eternal, are insignificant.

Were God not, the whole race of man would
be no better than the parasites that batten on
decay. But God is, and they who have best
insight best know that man's worth is meas-
ured by the degree of his kinship with Him,
without whom he would be but a semblance and
unreality.

If in any one of us there be aught that may
win approval or awaken admiration or thankfulness, whether it be truth, or honesty, or mildness,
or intelligence, or strength of mind, or rectitude,
or courage, or perseverance, or humility, or
love, or piety, or unselfishness, it is of, through,
and for God, from whom all life springs, to
whom all hope looks, toward whom all yearn-

ing moves, on whom all faith rests, in whom all hearts find repose.

In the twenty-five years on which we now set the seal of eternity, whatever may have been well done by any one of us has been done for Him and by His help. The field is His, the seed is His; His the rain and the sunshine; His the vital force that has built unto itself a body and brought about the harmonic play of all the members of the organism. We have been but His servants, and had we not been at all, He, had He so willed, would have found others and better. Our only merit is that of servants, and true service is our only blessedness.

The service we have chosen is that which the Eternal stooped to earth and wore human flesh to perform. It is the most beneficent, the holiest, the helpfullest, the most needful which it can fall to the lot of man to do. The task set us is to make ourselves and others Christ-like and God-like.

If those who profess to lead a religious life have the morals of the crowd or worse, they are the most contemptible and are, in fact, the most despised of men; but those who have the soul, and not merely the name of priest, are divine men — are, in word and deed, God's faithfullest witnesses to the Truth that liberates, to the Love that saves and beatifies.

" Whoso has felt the Spirit of the Highest
  Cannot confound nor doubt Him nor deny ;
  Yea, with one voice, O world, though thou deniest,
  Stand thou on this side, for on that am I."

No unworthy thought has impelled us to
commemorate this day with solemn rites and
grave words. Few of us are so immature as
to attach importance to a mere demonstration.
None of us are so frivolous as to imagine that
what is said of a man has meaning or value
other than that derived from what he is; and
what he is, not himself even, but God alone
knows.

There may be merit in collecting so many
thousand dollars and in paying mechanics for
fitting together so many stones and so many
pieces of wood, but where the aim and end are
spiritual, praise for doing such things is not to
the purpose. Neither the heart nor the proper
work of such a one is in matter, which has meaning for him only in so far as it is made to serve
higher interests, by becoming the nourishment
or the symbol of the soul. He knows that what
each one, and the social body as well, most needs
is not wealth, nor privilege, nor cunning, nor
favor, but larger, braver, holier, sweeter life —
more sympathy, more courage, more wisdom,
more love. Those prevail who are stronger than
their fellows — stronger through faith and de-

sire, through knowledge and virtue, through self-control and devotion to truth and justice. God is a Spirit, and those whose character is built on the principles which faith and hope make certain, which best reason approves, are the powers by which His reign is established and made perpetual. His servants conquer, not with the sword, not with money nor with the things money can buy, but by the soul, which, enrooted in Him, contemplates all things in the light of Eternity, and is calm and unmoved while the pomp and pageantry pass by to sink forever beyond the reach of all-penetrative thought. Men, like children, are attracted by a world of shows; they are busy with vanities, and attach importance to trifles. But from the central heart of religion the divine voice declares that only the things which minister to the soul's welfare have worth; that there is no genuine life but that which unfolds itself heavenward, and, like the tendril for the solid stem, reaches after God. Had we temples built of gold and adorned with every kind of precious stone; though the music of the masters, uttered by masters appealed to us; though from canvas and stone and high-raised pulpit genius spoke to us, it were all but show and sound if it did not lift the soul nearer to our Father in heaven. God's men are spiritual men, and the only religious progress is progress in faith and love, in wisdom and virtue.

What we commemorate to-day, we of the diocese of Peoria, bishops and priests, brothers and sisters, and the people whose servants we all are, what this company of distinguished men have come from many sees to help us to celebrate worthily, is our labors for the moralization, the purification, and the spiritualization of human life, is our devotion to the things that make for righteousness and peace and life everlasting.

If we have built churches, it is that the people may gather there, and through worship and the reception of the sacraments and the hearing of the Word may be refreshed, nourished, and renewed in their innermost being. If we have established schools, it is that the little ones, whom the blessed Saviour loved, who are our joy and our hope, may grow up in an atmosphere in which learning blends with piety, knowledge with faith, true thought with chaste life, love with obedience. If we have founded homes for those whom loss or sin or age or poverty has made helpless or miserable, it is because we know that they are our brothers and sisters, and that we do best for our Heavenly Father and for ourselves in serving them.

This is what we cherish most and most love.

If Peoria and the diocese of Peoria are dear to us, — and God and we all know they are, — it is so not chiefly for the beautiful site, the healthful climate, the fertile soil from which the corn bursts like song from happy hearts; it is so above all for the spirit of freedom, of good-will, of helpfulness, which breathes here as unhindered as the gentle wind that kisses the prairie into life and bloom; they are dear for the opportunity which is given here to all alike to upbuild character, to confirm will, to cultivate the mind, to follow after the better things of which faith and hope are the heralds.

If to-day for a moment, even in thought, I may separate myself from any one of those who during the twenty-five years that have now become a part of the unchangeable past have gathered about me in still increasing numbers and with hearts ever more willing, I will say that the affection I bear them and the joy they give me — which, like the ripening fruit and the mellowing wine, grow more precious as time lengthens — are born, not so much of the success with which they have accomplished whatever they have been asked to do, as of their spirit of disinterestedness and self-sacrifice, of their courage and ability, their magnanimity and single-heartedness, their never-slumbering watchfulness over the good name of the diocese

and that of its priesthood. When the office of
bishop was offered to me, if I hesitated to accept
the burden and the honor, it was largely (if my
memory deceive me not) from a dread lest my
opinion of man's high estate, as revealed in the
lives of priests and nuns, should be lowered by
the more intimate knowledge of them which
necessarily comes to those who are placed in
authority over them. A personal experience of
twenty-five years is a broad basis for the judgment of an individual, and it is a source of
inner strength and freedom to me to be able to
feel and to say, in perfect sincerity, that, though
priests and nuns are not exempt from the infirmities which inhere in all that is human, I have
found them to be the kindliest, the most unselfish, the most loyal, the most pure-minded, and
the most devoted of men and women. Never
have I appealed to them in vain, when I have
appealed to the God-like in man. They have
confirmed my faith in human nature, and in the
worth and sacredness of life.

They have made me more certain that we are
all the children of an Almighty and all-loving
Father, from out whose thought and care we
can never die.

Let me conclude, in my own name and in
that of the whole diocese, with the expression
of sincere thanks to his eminence, the Cardinal

Archbishop of Baltimore, to the most reverend archbishops and bishops, and to the reverend clergymen who have done us the honor to be our guests to-day and to heighten by their presence and sympathy the significance and the joy of this celebration.

VII.

EDUCATION AND PATRIOTISM.

AS they alone are Christians who strive earnestly to lead a high and worthy life, so only those who are seriously intent on making themselves wise, strong, and virtuous are patriots. Words are idle unless they are filled with meaning by the deeds of those who utter them. A soldier may die in battle, and be only a mercenary; but he who so lives as to make men thankful that he is their fellow-citizen is a patriot. By making use of the opportunities which liberty offers, one may amass vast wealth, and be an enemy of freedom; but he who frees himself from within by overcoming ignorance and greed makes us think well, not only of himself, but of his country also. Children love their parents, not when they praise them, but when by their intelligent and virtuous behavior they make them happy: and so those who boast of the greatness of their country do not therefore love it; but its true lovers are those who strengthen and glorify it by their wisdom, honesty, unselfishness, sincerity, and courage. If in a foreign land we see an American who is drunk, or loud and vulgar, we are forced to confess that he is not a true, but a false and traitorous American; and here at home the miserable victims of greed, who offer and take bribes, who combine to crush the weak, who to increase their trade make war on a defenseless people, are not true Americans, but false and traitorous Americans. The characteristics of a true American are good-will, sympathy with the helpless and oppressed, intelligence, uprightness, energy, courage, and industry; and if we love our country and desire to make its institutions permanent, we must labor to cultivate these virtues in ourselves and in those whom we are able to influence. The love of education, in the deep sense of the word, and the love of country are one and the same love. Nothing but education, domestic, religious, and scholastic, can form the virtues which make patriots.

Primarily, education is growth; and growth is made possible and promoted by nutrition. The food we take and assimilate makes us what we are. In the case of the body this is plain. We grow and maintain strength, by throwing day by day into the life-current the substances of which the body is composed. If this ceases,

we cease to grow and begin to decay. The taking of nourishment is not something which is
done once for all — it is a habitual process,
which goes on whether we eat or abstain,
whether we wake or sleep. This is also true
of our spiritual being. The mind grows by
what it feeds on habitually, day by day; and
the kind of nourishment it assimilates, and the
thoroughness with which it assimilates, determine its quality and power.

The proper nourishment of our spiritual being
is not knowledge or speculative truth. What
we merely know hardly enters into the fiber of
our higher nature. Hence the information we
get in school about the surface of the earth and
the stars, about kings and wars, about algebraic
and geometric problems, about philosophies and
literatures, neither makes a deep impression nor
is long remembered. Such information does
not so attract us as to cause us to live with it
and find in it our habitual nourishment. It
has therefore little to do with the formation of
character. When we ask what kind of man
one is, we do not mean to inquire about his
information or his possessions, but about his
character; and to get insight into his character we wish to learn, not what he knows, but
what in his inmost soul he believes, hopes, and
strives for — his tastes and preferences, his

bearing and behavior, the breadth and depth of his love, the largeness and fullness of his sympathies, his attitude toward the temporal and Eternal.

Thus character is primarily moral — it is what a man is, not the kind of clothes he wears or the kind of information he possesses. It is a result of nutrition and growth, and can nowise be formed by mechanical processes; and since character is the man himself, it is precisely this moral growth which it is the chief business of the school to promote; and if it fail in this, it fails radically. A characterless man is neither good in himself nor good in his relations to any part of the social environment. Character is formed by cultivating a taste for what is true, good, and fair, — a love for justice, honesty, and kindliness, for reverence, modesty, and courage; a loathing for dirt, physical and moral, in thought, word, and deed; a scorn of lies, hypocrisy, and cant, — by filling the young with profound faith in the worth and sacredness of life, by helping them to feel how divine a thing it is to be alive when one has hope and enthusiasm, is chaste and loving, wise and helpful. In learning to know their teachers the pupils should be able to perceive and love in them the fairest and noblest virtues. Heroic and saintly men and women also, as they are

portrayed in literature, should be often brought
before them. Thus they shall come to live not
only in an atmosphere of high thoughts, but
in the presence of the worthiest whom history
makes known; and they shall little by little
gain insight into the truth that life is more
than its circumstance, that right and honorable
life is the only prosperity, the only wealth, and
that the worst misfortune and punishment is to
be base. When the vital strength which issues
in right conduct has become habitual with them,
instinctive, a second nature, then we may urge
them with all confidence to build on this foundation whatever else may exalt, refine, and enrich human life; we may push them, according
to their endowments, to make themselves orators, poets, statesmen, captains of industry, men
of science, inventors, discoverers, leaders in religious and social movements, confident that the
more they upbuild their individual power the
more shall they become general benefactors and
true patriots, men who shall find their happiness
not in hoarding money, but in diffusing good,
in promoting religion, morality, education, and
whatever else tends to the common welfare.
Without misgivings we may seek to inspire
them with faith in the worth of intellectual
culture, with the confidence that they shall be
able to compass it, and with the love of the ex-

cellence which it procures. We may point out to them that the noblest work is that which man performs with his noblest faculties; that if the vicious are slaves, the ignorant are bond servants, fatally doomed to do the world's drudgery; that the chances of success, even in the ordinary affairs of life, are as two hundred and fifty to one, in favor of college-bred men and women. We may show them how a cultivated mind is a perpetual invitation and opportunity to raise one's self to higher and more profitable occupations, to acquaint one's self with the best thought contained in the best literature, and thus to make one's self at home with the noblest minds of all ages and countries; how in thus opening up an inexhaustible supply of spiritual nourishment, it gives one the freedom, not of a city, though the most glorious, but of the world, from the dawn of history, even to the present hour. We may go on to explain how much longer vigor of mind endures than vigor of body. The manual laborer is, I suppose, in his prime from the age of twenty-five to thirty-five years; he is old before he is fifty. The mental worker does not reach his prime before he is fifty, and, if he is a serious student, his value may increase till he is seventy and more. His period of growth (and growth is gladness) is very much longer

than that of the uneducated; and his work
has greater worth both for himself and for the
social environment.

If the average of moral and intellectual culture were higher, we should be able not only to
procure the needs and comforts of life with
less effort, but we should have the wisdom and
strength to deny ourselves many things which
are harmful and mere waste of individual and
collective force. All the luxuries involve dissipation of vital energy and deterioration of the
quality of life; but among the luxuries no sen-
sible man will place the great works of art,
which spring from the highest activities of the
soul, and without which our whole existence
must sink to lower levels. What more strik-
ing instance could there be of the crude kind
of thinking in vogue among us, than that a
university professor should deem it not absurd
to place a great money-gatherer on the same
footing with a great poet? The one is a mechanical, the other a vital man. Riches are
akin to fear, to cowardice and death; but the
highest thought rightly expressed is the fine
essence of the purest life stored up for all who
are able to appreciate and admire, even to the
remotest age.

But however high we may place genius
and intellectual culture as educational powers,

when there is question of patriotism we must
come back to the moral element in human
nature, to the sense of duty, to character. The
essential is not what we know, but what we
believe and love and do with all our hearts.
George Washington was not a man of genius
or of the best intellectual culture, but he was
a great character — honest, simple, true, disinterested, incorruptible. He thought not of
private gain, nor of personal glory, nor of the
aggrandizement of his country, but believing
with all his heart in the right of the people to
govern themselves, he gave his time, his wealth,
his life, to make such government actual and
permanent. It could not have occurred to him
that Americans should ever seek to conquer a
people struggling for independence — to him,
who had inscribed upon his victorious banner
the Declaration of Independence. He could not
have dreamed that the extension of trade and
the enriching of trusts should ever be deemed
by Americans a justification of wars of conquest. He had a noble soul, he had a great
heart, he had honest convictions, he had the
courage of his opinions. If we compare him
with Julius Cæsar, he is altogether inferior in
intellectual grasp and power, but wholly superior in character — in the qualities which make
a· man wise, helpful, and beneficent. The one

overthrew a Republic to build an empire, which quickly became the shame and ruin of the world; the other founded a republic which has been a refuge and blessing for all the victims of tyranny in the whole wide world, a republic for whose prosperity and continuance all pure, gentle, loving, and Christian souls in the whole wide world must pray.

VIII.

ASSASSINATION AND ANARCHY.

[Address delivered in Peoria at Mass-meeting in memory
of the death of President McKinley.]

IN the presence of the grief and humiliation
of a great nation, one would wish to be
silent. Words cannot give right utterance to
what we feel. They are apt even to strike us
as but noise and sound, to distract and disturb
rather than to strengthen and console. There
is not question here of the passing of a man,
however true, however good, however noble he
may have been. The occasion does not call for
clamorous denunciation or vulgar abuse; much
less for appeals to the beast of prey that ever
lurks in the human breast. Crime is not a
remedy for crime; lawlessness is not a correc-
tive of lawlessness. A great people and petty
thoughts or revengeful feelings go ill together.
The strong do not rail; the brave make no out-
cries. In proportion to one's power should be
his forbearance and self-control. If our dead
President was great, he was great through his

kindliness, his forgiving spirit, his desire to be
of help, his modesty and lowly-mindedness.
His greatness sprang from his Christian faith
and character, rather than from any surpassing.
intellectual endowments. If we grieve for his
sad taking away, let our thoughts and sentiments be such as he would approve. To die as
he died can hardly be deemed an evil for him.
For more than half a century he had led a life
of honesty, purity, and honor; he 'ad served
his God and his country from his earliest years;
he had reached the topmost height to which an
American citizen may aspire. He had the respect of the whole people; and those who dis-
agreed with him in matters of policy were glad
to accord him the high merit of a disinterested
patriotism. In the midst of a whole world
who thus honored him, while still in the full
vigor of manhood, untouched by the palsying
and blighting hand of age, he is suddenly
stricken by one whose mental and moral nature
had been wholly perverted. He dies in the fulfillment of kindly offices; he dies in the midst of
the people who loved him and whom he loved;
he dies after many years of life of noblest service and without stain. His task is done; his
fame is secure; and his example remains with
us to show us what a true American should be.

When the generous and the good have been

placed on the summit of earthly things, their memory abides as a possession forever. The calamity which has befallen, has befallen not him, but the nation. When dire misfortunes overtake individuals or a people whom inner power makes great, they convert what might utterly destroy baser natures to means of good. We shall therefore seek to find the uses there may be in this adversity. The cry of shame and rage which has been heard throughout the whole land is intelligible. It is the instinctive utterance of the love we bear our country and of the infinite abhorrence we feel for whoever or whatever may do it hurt. Within our inmost souls we are persuaded that America is God's greatest earthly gift to His children; that He has destined it to be the training ground of a nobler race, the home of a more Christlike and diviner humanity, whose beneficent influence shall be as self-diffusive as love, and as wide-spreading as the unending globe. When, therefore, a crime is committed against the one man who is the symbol and the representative of the whole national life, we are filled with amazement, we are confused with astonishment, we are roused to indignation, and in our mad bewilderment we lose sight of the fundamental principles on which our government rests. Declaimers and demagogues think to win favor by violent lan-

guage, and even from the chairs which have
been established to teach wisdom, rash counsels
are given.   When shall we acquire that repose
which is a mark of maturity, the imperturbable
mind which belongs to those who have faith in
an overruling Providence and are certain of
themselves?

There are no patent remedies for social evils.
What we sow we reap, whether there be question
of individuals or of nations. We cannot remain
habitually indifferent to the supreme interests
of religion and justice, and when emergencies
come upon us, save ourselves by devices and
contrivances.   We do not need more or new
laws: what we need is a new spirit — a more
real faith in God, a more real love of our fellow-
man, more honesty, more chastity, more unselfishness. We need a religion that will not lead
us to think it enough to skin and film the ulcer-
ous place, but that will impel us to probe deep
and cut away the gangrenous flesh that poisons
the fountains of life.

As a people we are wanting in respect for
those who are clothed with authority; we lack
reverence; we are too ready to persuade ourselves that all is well so long as wealth and population increase; we wish to be flattered, and we
turn away from the truth-speakers who love us,
to listen to the demagogues who would lure us

to ruin. We seek facile solutions of the great problems, and distrust whoever, for instance, declares that to teach the young to read, write, and cipher is not to educate them; that education consists essentially in the building of character, which is what a man is, and not what he knows. We forget that morality, and not legality, is the only foundation on which a free government can securely rest. When corrupt influences determine legislation, laws cease to be regarded as binding. Men yield to force, but in their hearts they rebel against. the injustice.

When immoralities and crimes become general, minds are perverted and consciences made callous. How is it possible to read day after day of the suicides, the murders, the lynchings, the robberies, the divorces, the adulteries, the prostitutions and corruptions with which the newspapers are filled, and not to lose the sense of the sacredness of human life?

Vice propagates itself far more easily than virtue, as men take disease, but not health, from one another; and if whoever is guilty of crime, or of misdeeds of whatever kind, is at once advertised to the world in millions of sheets as an object of curiosity, of interest, and at times of admiration, how can the readers of such things retain balance of judgment and a sensitive consciousness of the heinousness of sin?

It is easy to put to death the wretched man
who has committed the outrage which has filled
us all with consternation; it is easy to denounce
and difficult to exaggerate the inhumanity, the
fiendish nature of those who would destroy the
whole fabric of society, our very civilization,
the beliefs, the laws, the forces, which make us
men and give value to life; it is easy in the hour
of national affliction to gather in numerous as-
semblies throughout the land to utter our grief
and to express our abhorrence. And all this is
well, springing as it does from what is best
within us; but it has little efficacy. It will do
good only if it helps to make us good. We cannot destroy anarchy by enacting more rigid
laws; much less by resorting to violence.

"God bless every undertaking," said President McKinley in 1897, "God bless every
undertaking which revives patriotism and re-
bukes the indifferent and lawless." And in
1894: "With patriotism in our hearts there is
no danger of anarchy and no danger to the
American Union."

There is the patriotism of instinct, that which
binds a man to the land of his birth and to the
home about which cluster his earliest and sweet-
est memories; and there is the patriotism of
reason and religion, whereby we are made conscious that our dearest interests, temporal and

eternal, are vitally associated with our country, with its prosperity and security, its honor and welfare. The patriotism of instinct needs little encouragement; it is implanted by nature and is self-developed; but that of reason and religion must be cultivated and cherished with ceaseless care and vigilance, as reason and religion themselves are living forces only in the self-active.

To this higher patriotism none but the wise and good are true; and false to it are not those alone who commit crime against the majesty and sacredness of the State, but false to it are all who are vicious themselves, all who by word or example sow the seeds of vice. The germ of anarchy is in every wrongdoer, in every law-breaker. It is in those who propagate irreligion, who undermine man's faith in God and in his own spiritual nature, for the moral code of the people is their religion. What is right or wrong for them is what they believe, not what they know, to be so. For all of us, indeed, duty is a thing of faith, not of the pure reason. Religion has rocked the cradles of all the nations, and infidelity, issuing in insatiable greed and sensuality, has dug the graves of those that have perished, sophistry and indulgence destroying what had been built by faith and virtue. There is the principle of anarchy in the mobs

that gather to torture and murder with fiendish
cruelty the unfortunate beings for whose punishment laws have been enacted. There is the
germ of anarchy in the homes of those who
marry as recklessly, and separate with as little
compunction, as animals breed. It is in the
boodleism which in our cities fosters prostitution, the criminal saloon, the dance hall, and the
gambling den. It is in our street fairs, when
they are made a pretext for pandering to the
lowest passions of the crowd. It lurks in the
very constitution of our competitive system, if
this system leads us to prefer markets to men,
riches to the dignity and honor of human beings;
if it so turns us away from the ends and ideals
for which the wise live as to make of the nation
a money-getting mob, where the few are dwarfed
and crippled by their enormous possessions,
while the multitude seek to drown their sense of
misery in alcohol and degrading pleasures. It
is not conceivable that this should be the fate
of us, the heirs of all ages, us, the latest birth
of time. Rather shall we lay to heart and be
convinced in our inmost souls of this truth,
uttered by one of the best inspired teachers of
our age: " There is no wealth but life — life,
including all its powers of love, of joy, and of
admiration. That country is the richest which
nourishes the greatest number of noble and

happy human beings; that man is richest who, having perfected the functions of his own life to the utmost, has also the widest helpful influence, both personal and by means of his possessions, over the lives of others."

There is not now, nor has there ever been, a civilized people. Ignorance, sin, depravity, injustice, cruelty, deceit, greed, and selfishness have always prevailed and still prevail in the world. The majority has never loved, nor does it now love, truth and mercy and purity and holiness. But we, more than any other people, are dedicated to the securing of the largest freedom, the fullest opportunity. the completest justice to all — to men and women, to the strong and the weak, to the rich and the poor. These are the principles which we proclaimed when first we took our place in the family of Christian nations; these are the principles which our greatest and most representative men, whether orators or statesmen or warriors or poets, have with deepest conviction asserted to be the embodiment of the spirit of America. This is the meaning of our life; this is the key to our destiny. Our conception of democracy is not that it is, like some of the barbarian empires of the past, an irresistible power whose mission is to overrun and subjugate, to conquer and lay waste. On the contrary, from our point of view democracy

is a beneficent force. It rests on faith in human
nature; on the educability of all men, if they be
but rightly environed and attended.

Institutions are preserved by the principles
from which they originate, and if our country
is to grow, not in wealth and numbers alone,
but in inner power and worth, we must adhere
with unalterable fidelity to the great truths
which inspired our fathers when they founded
the Republic. Nay, since it is the nature of vital
truth to develop, we must see more clearly than
it was possible for them to see, that the Republic
means justice to all, good-will to all, helpfulness
to all; and first of all, to those who are overburdened, who are insufficiently equipped, who are
sorely tried. The cry of the laborer is for justice, not for charity; and it is a cry which all
the good gladly reëcho. But let us remember
that men are just only when they love. Sympathy gives insight, and where this is lacking
we are blind to the injustice our fellows suffer
and we do them wrong with easy consciences.
The impulse now, as of old, is to seek to overcome evil with evil. The world is so full of perversity that the only way, it would seem, in
which society can protect itself is to cut off
for a time or for ever those who sin against its
laws. But no punishment, however severe, can
destroy the roots from which grows the tree

that bears the bitter fruit; and if in any part of the world men should ever become rightly civilized, they will overcome evil with good. They will not condemn men to do work which they cannot do with joy, work which takes away heart and hope, which cripples the body and darkens the mind. They will suffer none to live in ignorance who might have knowledge; none to live in vice who might be made pure and holy. In their cities there will not be found districts where no innocent or healthful creature can breathe and not become tainted. There shall be no fortunes built on dead men's bones and cemented with blood; no splendid dwellings around which shriek the ghosts of women whose toil did not bring enough to save them from lives of shame. It is toward all this that we must strive and struggle, if we are not to be recreant to our most sacred duties, false to the mission which God has given to America.

In the shadow of the gloom that falls on the hearts of all the people, as what was mortal of the most religious, the most God-fearing of our presidents is lowered into the grave, let the eternal principles of freedom and justice, of truth and love, of religion and righteousness, gleam on us with fuller beauty and power, like stars from the raven bosom of night.

Let us rouse ourselves from the torpor which

benumbs our spiritual being. Let us forget a little our petty and selfish interests and pleasures, that we may become able to enter into the larger life of our country, each working as a separate individual force for the good of all. So shall the calamity which has befallen startle us into newness of heart and mind, making us more solicitous for the common welfare, more careful lest we ourselves give offense; so shall there be more love and piety in our homes, more reverence and docility in our schools, more faith and religion in our churches, more wisdom and virtue in our public life. And in this way, and possibly in no other, shall we be able to make such crimes as this, which has filled us with horror and dismay, for ever impossible.

IX.

CHURCH AND COUNTRY.

WHEN a bishop gets an auxiliary it is time for him to begin to grow silent, even though in our councils we have declared that a bishop's chief office and duty is to preach. But, as the steed that has been familiar with the gleam of bayonets and the thunder of battle will still, amid the peaceful fields and quiet homes of men, at the faintest breath of some martial strain, feel again the warlike fire rekindle, so indeed it would be hard for me to keep silence when you ask me to speak of the things which for many years I have tried to love best — the Catholic Church and the American Republic. Are they not the symbols of what should be most dear to true and well-born souls — the love of God and the love of one's fellow-men?

It is a habit with us to speak of the triumphs and glories of the Church in ages which are gone. We love to tell the story of her martyrs and confessors, of her saints and founders of religious orders; we dwell gladly on her mar-

velous success in converting the barbarous
races that have grown into Christendom, in
purifying morals, in softening manners, in con-
secrating and protecting woman, in founding
schools, in preserving the treasures of classical literature, in fostering the arts; in leading
migratory tribes to choose fixed homes, to fell
the forest, drain the marsh, build cities and put
themselves under the rule of law. Her name
has indeed been associated at times, during the
lapse of nineteen hundred years, with things
upon which we cannot dwell with pleasure or approval, but her general course and influence have
made for righteousness, peace, charity, reverence,
chastity, obedience, mildness, modesty, kindliness, and habits of cheerful industry. What she
has been able to do in other ages and other lands
she is still able to do for us here and now; and
though we rise in dignity of being in proportion to our power to live in thought in the past
and the future, yet since life is chiefly action,
our first concern is with the present. In the
Church there is an exhaustless fountain-head of
spiritual energy, since in her, as the Saviour
has taught us to believe, there abides the very
Spirit of God. But if this energy is to manifest itself in the world, it can only be through
God-like men. To such it was intrusted in the
beginning, by such it was spread throughout

the earth, and by such alone can its divine healing be communicated to the sick and hungering
souls of the people. On us it depends whether
the sacred ark shall ride in safety, bearing the
holiest and most priceless treasures, on the rising waters of the modern democracy; whether
again as of old, the priest shall not merely point
the way to heaven, but be also a pioneer in all
the paths that lead to wider knowledge, truer
freedom, and more wholesome living.

Now, all the great things that mold and
transform human life — religion, patriotism,
friendship, love, devotion to heroic men and
right causes — must be cared for and followed
for themselves, and with all one's mind and
heart, or their power to strengthen, uplift, and
purify is lost. Shall we, the leaders of the
Church in America, be able to turn resolutely
from the false lights of momentary success, of
material progress, of pride in mere numbers
and showy buildings, to the inner sources of
power, to knowledge and wisdom, to purity
and love, to modesty and mildness? Shall we
be able to free ourselves from the awful pressure of a public opinion which believes in nothing but money — and shrewdness as a means
to money — an opinion that

> " Hangs upon us with a weight
> Heavy as frost and deep almost as life " ?

Shall we be able to reach and maintain a living and passionate faith in an estate higher than that of men — a faith which shall make us reverent, devout, patient, and self-denying; which shall impel us to desire and labor for the things that lead to life, and to put far away the things that lead to destruction? If so, then in making ourselves worthy to be called ministers of Him who died for all, we shall find that we have become capable of rendering the highest services to the State of which we are citizens.

If we do not work for bread with our hands, we are bound under penalty of becoming criminal, to labor with brain and heart, to strengthen, purify, and enrich human life; and the basest of those who fail in this are the false shepherds of souls, who, having pledged themselves to the care and nurture of the spirit, sink into indolence and ignorance, while the people perish of inanition or are devoured by the beast of prey that lurks in each one's bosom. There must be work of hand that men may live, and there must be work of brain and heart that they may live worthily and nobly. It is not necessary that we should live, but it is necessary that, being alive, we should live well; and hence the tasks intrusted to the scholars, the teachers, and the priests of a people are the highest and most indispensable. The desire to teach, to teach those who do not know it, the truth that is freedom, the knowledge that is power, the wisdom that is peace and joy, lies at the heart of the purest and divinest yearnings to be of help; and therefore the greatest teachers have been and are the chief lovers and benefactors of the race.

In whom should this yearning, as of a god, be found if not in the Catholic priest whose good fortune it is to labor for the salvation of the souls and the temporal welfare of men in the American Republic?

What has such power to make the noblest efforts at once possible and effectual as the consciousness of living in the midst of a free, generous, and brave people? What inducement to make ourselves more and more fit for the work we have chosen is so powerful as the sense of success in accomplishing the task? What is so good as to follow after high aims in the midst of a people who are more alive than men are elsewhere on earth?

In many ways our country is dear to men of many minds. Like a most richly endowed soul, it has gifts for all who are not unworthy. The millions who have been bound in the triple chains of servitude, poverty, and ignorance feel, as they put their feet on our shores and breathe our air, that the night is past and the dawn is come. Here opportunity beckons, here occasion waits, here hope invites, here the general condition of things urges us to make ourselves men.

Where else shall we find, I will not say, so much tolerance, — for tolerance implies evil, implies necessity, implies indifference, — but so much good-will, so much loving-kindness, so great readiness to go to the help of the weak and suffering? Where else is so much light thrown upon the whole life of the people? And however offensive and even harmful the glare which the public press flashes upon evil deeds may be, yet is light not only the best policeman, but the chief purifier and quickener, the most fatal foe of filth and disease, whether of body or of soul. Where else are all men so given to the ways and arts of peace, so little crazed by the bray of trumpets and the glitter of steel, so little blinded by the flame of war-like glory, which is fed by the gases of the putrescent bodies of the slain?

We have no dynasty to defend with our blood, no empire to be held together by great standing armies, no religious quarrels which we think it possible to settle by wager of battle; yet is there no danger that we shall become effeminate, for it requires a higher and truer courage to live for one's country in a right spirit than to die for it on the field of carnage.

Where else is there a people so eager to learn, so confident in the power of education to transform individual and social life, so quick to test whatever new thing may give promise of help? Where else is property so safe, well-being so widely diffused, woman so educated and honored? Reasons enough, indeed, these are for loving our country; but those who love may not be free from watchful and anxious care, and the more priceless the treasure, the more vigilant should be its guardians. History is full of the stories of fallen republics. Those of Athens and Rome and Venice flourished, and then fell to ruin. Shall our own have the same fate, or shall it, obedient to the heart prayer and inmost desire of all noble souls, endure while its mountains stand and its rivers flow?

Only truth can make and keep individuals free, and righteousness alone can serve as an everlasting foundation of national liberty. In vain our numbers multiply, in vain our wealth accumulates, in vain our lines of commerce weave themselves into a network that enmeshes the globe, if we ourselves decay, if we lose firm grasp of the spiritual verities which constitute the worth and honor of human life. There are doubtless signs of degeneracy on many sides, nor is there in this cause for surprise.

We have been successful to a marvelous degree; and the tendency of success is to nourish conceit and to undermine good sense. We have become the richest of the nations; and it is the tendency of wealth to corrupt and harden the heart. A great English writer says of Americans: " This is their specialty; this their one gift to their race — to show men how not to worship, how never to be ashamed in the presence of anything "; and in so far as there is truth in his words, the source of the evil is to be sought for chiefly in our uninterrupted success and in our fabulous wealth. We are tempted to consider the authority of gold as higher than the authority of God, and a man's circumstances as more important than the man himself.

Are not the foundations of the home growing weaker, and has not our popular education failed to accomplish much that we had most earnestly hoped for and expected? " The idea of a general education," says Ruskin, " which is to fit everybody to be Emperor of Russia, and provoke a boy, whatever he be, to want to be something else, and wherever he was born to think it a disgrace to die, is the most entirely and directly diabolic of all the countless stupidities into which the British nation has of late been betrayed by its avarice and irreligion." In this matter, at least, there seems to be something like an alliance between the British nation and the American people.

But true thoughts are thoughts that inspire hope and courage; and whatever leads us to think meanly of ourselves or of our country is to be put away as evil. Good men, like good books, are those that fill us with confidence in the triumph of truth and justice and love, and so help us to conquer in the battle against doubt and sensuality and greed. Great souls are brave souls, and the wise understand that it is better to find fault with one's self than with one's country or one's age. There is no joy but in strength—strength of body, strength of mind, strength of heart. Weakness is the true opposite of virtue, which, if it be not strength, loses its name and essence. If we would influence and improve men, if we would ourselves grow better, we should cherish brave thoughts, speak brave words, do brave deeds. If we are lovers and doers of good, we must make ourselves also amiable; for else we shall easily teach men to distrust or even to hate the best things. The unlovableness of the pious does more harm to religion than the mocking of infidels.

For myself, the more I learn to know the

past, the more confident I become that God is still leading His children to higher and holier things. It is His world, and not the devil's. He is with us, and why should we grow despondent or afraid? I envy none but the young, but those who in the full vigor of early manhood salute the century that now opens the gates of a wider and fairer future for mankind. Wordsworth, standing on the threshold of the nineteenth century, when all men's minds were aglow with thoughts and hopes of liberty and fraternity, exclaimed:

> "Bliss was it in that dawn to be alive,
> But to be young was very heaven."

Nor was he wrongly inspired; for though our century has not accomplished all that the poet dreamed, yet when its history is summed, it shall stand forth as the one in which the Christian peoples made the greatest and most real progress in knowledge, in freedom, and in power. Had we nothing to set to its account but the growth and consolidation of the American Republic and the revivification and spread of the Catholic religion throughout the English-speaking world, it were enough. And when I am tempted to envy the young, and to cry out that youth be given me again, it is not that I may be bathed afresh, as in my early days, in the golden light of new-born worlds, when all the hills were clothed in mystic hues and all the valleys filled with flowers, when the earth itself seemed ready to break forth into a universal shout of joy, into an all-bewitching smile of beauty. Not for this, nor for the free heart and the mind at ease that recreate a paradise, would I be young again, but that I might bend the full force of pristine vigor to the upbuilding of my own being; that I might reduce my whole endowment to faculty, and having made myself a man, might devote myself to the service of the Catholic religion and the American Republic in the new century, which bears omens of mightier conflicts and nobler triumphs than men have ever known.

X.

LABOR AND CAPITAL.

THE people of America have many things
to be thankful for. The material resources of our country are so great that as yet
neither we nor the world at large have been
able to measure their extent. Hidden storehouses of wealth are continually being revealed to us. We are energetic, industrious,
brave, and untiring. We are convinced of the
supremacy of mind over matter, and we make
ceaseless and increasing efforts to educate the
spiritual faculties of the whole people. We are
averse to war and believe that disputes between nations, as between individuals, should
be settled by discussion and arbitration. We
are opposed to standing armies, believing that
the national wealth and intelligence should be
devoted to the improvement and culture of the
citizens, and not to conquest and destruction.
We have no powerful neighbor to repel or overthrow. Our comparative exemption from war
has made possible the rapid development of our

country. The love of peace, which is a characteristic of the American people, manifests itself also in religious good-will and toleration. As dynastic wars are for us out of the question, so are religious wars. The spirit of forbearance and helpfulness manifests itself in our customs and habits as in our legislation. In no other country is property more secure; in no other is it so generally diffused. Nowhere else is opportunity for woman as for man so universal; nowhere is there such faith in the national destiny; nowhere has the fusion of peoples differing in many and important respects been brought about so rapidly or so satisfactorily; nowhere are the multitudes so eager to learn or so quick to avail themselves of new discoveries and inventions. The millions from foreign lands who have founded homes here are making other millions in the Old World thankful that America exists. We are indeed a source of hope and confidence to all, in whatever part of the earth, who love justice and liberty, who believe in a higher and more blessed social and religious future for mankind. Already we are the possessors of greater wealth than any other nation possesses or has ever possessed; and though a few men, whose names stare us in the face from the pages of the newspapers, have fortunes that seem almost fabulous, there is diffused among the masses of the people a well-being and comfort such as exists in no other land. This may be perceived in the housing of the people, in their clothing, in the wholesomeness of their food, and above all in the spirit of courage and hopefulness which pervades our whole life.

There is no gulf between the rich and the poor, but a gradation of generally distributed possessions.

Nevertheless it is obvious that when there is question of American life, a merely optimistic view is a shallow and false view. There are great and widespread evils among us, as also tendencies which if allowed to take their course will lead to worse evil. There is the universal political corruption. There is the diminished sense of the sacredness of property. There is the loosening of the marriage tie and the sinking of the influence of the home. There is a weakening of the power to apprehend spiritual truth, and a consequent lowering of the standards of value, a falling away from the vital principles of religion, even while we profess to believe in religion. There is, indeed, enough and more than enough to keep all who cherish exalted ideas of the worth of human life and who love America lowly-minded and watchful.

One of the most certain signs of decadence

is a failure of the will, and one might think that we are threatened with this. Our ability to react against abuses is growing feebler. The social organism is so vast and so complex that it seems hopeless to attempt to interfere, and so we permit things to take their course, abdicating the freedom and the power of will in the presence of an idol which we call Destiny. The more public opinion is shaped by the ideals of evolution as the supreme law of life, the less capable we become of bringing reason and conscience to bear on human affairs, of recognizing God's presence in the world, and holding to truth and love as something higher and mightier than a universe of matter.

The course of things is, indeed, but partially subject to human control. Human progress nevertheless depends chiefly on human intelligence and energy, which, if they cannot create, can shape and guide. The one means of promoting the welfare of man is labor or effort. It alone can develop his mind, can form his character, can protect him from the blind forces of nature, and provide for him what is necessary for his comfort and dignity. The end of labor is the strengthening and enrichment of life, and the best measure of its value is the effect it produces on man, individually and collectively. The end is not abundance of riches, but noble life, healthful, pure, intelligent, brave, and loving. No wealth can enrich the brutal and the base; no possessions can purchase joy or peace for the slaves of appetite. Where right human life is led, — a life of faith, hope, and love, of thought and self-control, of industry and self-denial, — to live with as few material and animal wants as possible ennobles man. To learn to live with as little as possible and to waste nothing that is needful is the sum of practical wisdom. Socrates was happy in thinking how many things the world is full of which he did not need. Simple pleasures are the best. Expensive luxuries harm those who indulge in them, and bring misery to many. The highest ambition springs not from the desire to rise in the world, but from the will to lead an honest helpful life, whatever one's circumstances. One may be a wise, good, and happy man, or a foolish, wicked, and miserable man, whether rich or poor. We must have food, shelter, and clothing that we may live; but we should live not to be fed and housed, but to grow in knowledge and virtue, in helpfulness and holiness.

For the most fortunate men life is full of difficulties and troubles; for the poorest it may be filled with light, peace, and blessedness.

To be a man is to think as well as to work,

and the more intelligence there is in the work the better shall it be for the workers.

Reason as well as religion impels those who work with the head and those who work with the hands to coöperation, not to conflict. The interests of both are best served when they are friends. If labor is not directed by ability it is sterile. The notion that those who work with the hands are the sole producers of wealth is a fallacy which should deceive no one. The vast increase of wealth in the modern world of industry and commerce is the result to a far greater degree of ability than of labor. It has been produced chiefly by the comparatively few men of exceptional gifts, who have invented machines, organized enterprises, opened markets, and thus given work and sustenance to millions who but for them would never have been born. Capital itself, which makes our great undertakings feasible, is largely stored ability — ability embodied and made permanently fruitful in the means of production and distribution. Columbus did not sail his ships, but had it not been for his genius they would not have sailed at all; and had the mutinous crew thrown him overboard, they would have drifted to death and the New World had not been discovered. The natural sources of wealth had existed in America for countless ages, but the savages who dwelt here lived in poverty and wretchedness because they lacked men of ability to lead them to the conquest of the riches of whose existence they were ignorant.

Capital is like an exquisite musical instrument — valueless if there is no one who knows the secret of its uses, and the men of ability who know how to use capital wisely are as rare as excellent musicians. Laborers may be compared to soldiers, who conquer only when they are disciplined, equipped, and commanded by men of ability. It has been calculated that two-thirds of the wealth produced in the nineteenth century were due to ability, and but one-third to the work of those who toil with their hands. This applies to spiritual not less than to material wealth. The great advances of mankind, in whatever sphere, have been made through the genius and under the leadership of a few highly endowed individuals — the prophets of better things, the subduers of the foes of man, the pioneers of progress. Land and labor are the primary sources of wealth, but its production in the modern world is due chiefly to ability, working with capital, which it more than any other agency has created. Nothing is more wonderful than the hand, but its almost miraculous power is due to the fact that it is the instrument of the brain.

In former times the men of ability were drawn to devote themselves to war or government or philosophic speculation, but now more than ever before they throw themselves into industry and commerce, making the pursuit of riches their life-aim. This is the career which seems to promise the most immediate and the most substantial results; and the really able men are so few and the work to be done is so immeasurable and so complex, that the demand for these exceptional individuals is greater than the supply. Every great enterprise, every great business concern, needs for its success what they alone can give. Hence they command salaries which seem to be exorbitant; hence they grow rich, become capitalists and form combinations of capital, which appear to many to be a menace to the freedom and welfare of the whole people. Competition, which begins as a struggle for existence, finally becomes a desire to crush and dominate, becomes a warfare, which if less bloody is not less horrible or cruel than that which is carried on with shot and shell. As in battle the generals, however humane they be, think only of victory and are heedless of the suffering and the loss of life, so in the struggle for industrial and commercial supremacy, the men of ability, the leaders and capitalists are wholly bent on the attainment of their ends, and easily lose sight of the principles of justice and humanity.

It is this that makes the organization of workmen into labor- and trades- unions inevitable and indispensable. The consciousness that if they do not protect and defend themselves they will be ground by the wheels of a vast machine or reduced to a condition little better than that of slaves, compels them to unite lest they be deprived of the common rights of man. In ancient times laborers were slaves, it is not long ago since multitudes of them in our own country were slaves; and however the fact be disguised, the natural tendency of greed, of the love and pursuit of material things as the chief good of life, is to deaden the sense of justice and humanity, to make the strong, the men of ability, feel that they have the right to do whatever they are able to do. They are not necessarily unjust or cruel, but they become the victims of a false belief and the agents of a system which is as pitiless as a law of nature.

One of the chief forces by which this tendency is held in check is the religious principle and feeling that men are the children of God, and have inalienable rights; that work should enable the worker to lead a life not unworthy of a rational being; that riches which are procured at the cost of human misery and degradation are accursed; that what constitutes the proper value of individuals and of nations is spiritual and not material; that there is eternal wrath in store for all who trample upon moral and intellectual good that they may add to their possessions. These truths are accepted by the public opinion of the civilized world, and hence there is a general sympathy with laborers in their efforts to obtain justice and to improve their condition. All who observe and reflect recognize that their lot is hard, that they bear an undue share of the burdens of life, that they are often forced to do work which is destructive of health and happiness, and that they are exposed to greater vicissitudes of fortune than others.

All this, however, would accomplish little for their improvement if they themselves remained indifferent, if they did not organize, if they did not discuss and come to a fuller consciousness of their grievances, if they did not by strikes and other lawful means make strenuous efforts to increase their wages or to prevent them from falling, if they did not agitate for fewer hours of work and whatever else may give them leisure and opportunity to cultivate their spiritual natures and thus to make themselves capable of enjoying life in a rational and Christian way. Economic laws, which are immutable,

make it impossible that wages should rise beyond a given point, or that wealth should be
so distributed as to make all men rich. The
multitude are poor and can never be rich. It
is indeed fortunate that it is impossible that the
masses of mankind should ever be able to lead
an idle and luxurious life. It is a law of human
nature that man shall work and abstain, if it
is to be well with him; that to do nothing and
enjoy much is impossible. Political Economy,
like government, rests on a basis of morality.
Moral character alone can give a man self-respect, courage, hope, cheerfulness, and power
of endurance. Hence the laborers, and all who
identify themselves with their cause, should
have a care first of all that they be true men —
provident, self-restrained, kindly, sober, frugal,
and helpful; and that this may be possible, also
religious. The foe of labor is not capital, but
ignorance and vice. In the whole English-
speaking world, at least, its worst enemy is
drink. More than a combination of all employers, the saloon has power to impoverish
and degrade workingmen. In their own ranks
the traitors are those who preach irreligion and
anarchy. The influence of Christianity has
been and is the chief power which has brought
the world to recognize the rights of the en-
slaved, the poor, the weak, of all who are heavy-

laden and over-burdened. It aroused and it alone can sustain enthusiasm for humanity. If this faith could die out, what would remain but the law of the survival of the fittest, that is, of the strongest, the most unscrupulous, the most reckless of the sufferings and sorrows of their fellow-men? These are the men who prosper among savages, in barbarous states, and in periods of anarchy.

But it is not conceivable that the civilized world should turn from the principles which Christ proclaimed, whose development and diffusion must in the end substitute for universal competition — the war of all upon all — the co-operation of all with all, not merely or chiefly for the winning of the bread that nourishes the body, but above all for the spread of the higher life of truth and love, of purity and goodness. In America, assuredly, we have good reason to take a hopeful view of the future. No foreign power can offer hindrance to our progress in the fulfillment of our God-given tasks, which are not only to secure equal rights, liberties, and opportunities to all the people, but so to educate and inspire all the inhabitants of this great continent that they may all work together to shape here a nobler manhood and womanhood than the world has ever seen.

XI.

WORK AND LEISURE.

L IFE is energy: we feel ourselves only in
doing, and when we inquire what a man's
value is we ask what is his performance. The
deed is the proof of faith, the test of character,
and the standard of worth. To do nothing is to
be nobody, and to have done is to have been.
True work fixes attention, develops ability, and
enriches life; it strengthens the mind, forms the
will, and inures to patience and endurance. It
is what we do and suffer to overcome nature's
indifference and hostility to man's well-being
and progress; it is the means whereby what is
not ourselves is taken hold of and made to do
us service. True work, then, is furtherance of
life, and it cannot be rightly understood unless
it be looked at in this light. To know the worth
of work we must consider first of all what is its
effect upon the worker. If it warps, cripples,
and degrades him it is not true work, though
he should thereby amass vast wealth or gain
great reputation. That work is best which helps

to make men and women wise and virtuous; and that which breeds vice is worst, is little better than idleness, which is evil because it breeds vice. The political and social conditions which are most favorable to work that elevates and enriches and purifies human life approach nearest to the ideal; the political and social conditions which involve the physical deterioration and the mental and moral degradation of multitudes are barbarous, and unless they are improved must lead to the ruin of the State. From this point of view, which is the only true point of view, our present economic and commercial systems are subversive of civilization. They sacrifice men to money; wisdom and virtue to cheap production and the amassing of capital. They foster greed in the stronger and hate in the weaker. They drive the nations to competitive struggles which are as cruel as war, and in the final result more disastrous; for their tendency is to make the rich vulgar and heartless, and the poor reckless and vicious. As stratagems and lies are considered lawful in war, so in the warfare of commercial competition opinion leans to the view that whatever may be done with impunity is right. The adulteration of food and drink, the watering of stocks, the bribing of legislators, the crushing of weaker concerns, the enforced idleness of

thousands who are thereby driven to despair
and starvation, are not looked upon as lying
within the domain of morals, any more than the
shooting of man in battle is considered a question of morality. The degradation and ruin
of innumerable individuals are implications of
the law of competition, just as in the struggle
for existence there is a world-wide crushing and
destruction of the weak by the strong. On the
other hand, the capitalists, the captains in the
armies of laborers, are, under the present system, driven like the workmen themselves. The
necessity of ceaseless vigilance and effort keeps
them under continual strain. Like those they
employ, they become parts of a machine, and
therefore partial and mechanical men. The
sense of inner freedom dies within them, the
source of the purest joy runs dry, and they are
made incapable of thinking great thoughts or
of walking in the light of high ideals. They
are the victims of their own success, and, having great possessions, are poor in themselves.
The work, then, which we are doing, and the
conditions under which we are doing it, whether
we be rich or poor, are unfavorable to the best
kind of life.

We are the slaves instead of being the masters
of our work; we have forgotten that work is
a means and not an end; as the money for which

we work is a means and not an end. Believing
that work and riches are the ends of life, we
work with feverish hurry, and our greed grows
as our possessions increase. God, says Eurip-
ides, hates busy-bodies and those who do too
much. We are too busy, we do too much. And
the temper our restless activity creates makes
us incapable of leisure, which is the end of
work. The man is worth, not what his work is
worth, but what his leisure is worth. By his
work he gains a livelihood, but his leisure is
given him that he may learn how to live, that
he may acquire a taste for the best things, may
acquaint himself with what is truest and most
beautiful in literature and art, in science and
religion, may come to a knowledge of how he
may find himself, not chiefly in the narrow
circles of his private interests, but in the wide
world of noble thought and generous emotion.
For every man who rises above the vulgar life
is divided into two parts, the one to be devoted
to means, the other to ends. On the one side
he places the things of practical concern, — trade,
business, and politics; on the other the things
which are ends in themselves, — the upbuilding
of his own being with the help of religion, philosophy, science, and art. Whoever permits the
occupations whereby he gains a livelihood to
absorb his whole thought and energy is neces-

sarily an incomplete man. He lacks openness
of mind, breadth of view, the sense of beauty,
and the disinterested love of knowledge. His
perception of spiritual truth is dimmed, and he
is made incapable of the purest and most generous emotions. To give him something of all
this, leisure, if rightly used, may serve; and
hence I say the man is worth what his leisure
is worth.

But who makes a wise use of leisure? The
pleasures to which it is devoted are dissipations
rather than recreations. The theatre might be
a school of refinement and taste, but it is, in
fact, rather a school of coarseness and vulgarity.
As for the club, Cicero said, nearly two thousand years ago, that those who have no love of
study join clubs. The dinner habit is as fatal
to physical and moral health as the newspaper
habit is to intellectual culture. Sir William
Temple thought life would be endurable were it
not for its pleasures; and so our busy Americans feel that it would be bearable were it not
for its leisures, in which they bore and are
bored.

As for those who do the rough work of the
world, fewer hours of toil will hardly be of benefit to them, if their leisure be spent in saloons
and in the company of the vicious. Work
must be done, — work of hand, that we may

have the means of living; work of head, that our life may be worth having; and this is the nobler work. A man's importance is determined by his usefulness, and the most useful are not those who provide food for the body, but those who nourish and exalt the spiritual faculties; as the greatest people is not the richest people, but the people that has the greatest number of noble, generous, fair, and enlightened men and women. Such men and women are found only where leisure is looked upon as a heavenly gift, as an opportunity to upbuild one's being, to prepare one's self for complete living.

XII.

THE MYSTERY OF PAIN.

Put pain from out the world, what room were left
For thanks to God, for love to man?
                                        — *Browning.*

THERE is hope and courage in the air of America. No other people has carried optimism to such extremes. We refuse to listen to talk of failure, or to entertain despondent thoughts, holding nothing impossible. This splendid confidence is found not alone in our attitude toward material things. In brief time we have subdued a continent and amassed incredible wealth, but we feel certain that we shall be able also to overcome ignorance, poverty, crime, and evil of whatever kind. We believe that this is God's world and that we are His most fortunate children. Is not America a happy land, where good and better days are now, and yet to come?

If we cannot shut our eyes to sorrow and misery we look to find in them some soul of goodness. As darkness is light's relief, death

life's foil, so we like to think that evil exists
that we may be impelled to learn to know and
love the truth and beauty which are everywhere.
In our optimism there is doubtless something
of the Israelite's satisfaction with this present
world, of his delight in a land flowing with milk
and honey; but there is also in it much of his
moral earnestness, of his belief in righteousness, in work done well and done in a Godlike
spirit. We are not dreamers, but doers; and
genuine doers are brave and cheerful and confident. Those who feel it were better never to
have been born, feel too that to do nothing is
happiness. But for us he who does nothing is
nobody; and in our deepest heart we understand
that those alone who act in obedience to the
voice of duty really do anything worth while:
the essential good being moral and religious,
nothing else having power to create in the
human breast a harmonious world or to give
lasting joy to man.

The things which have value are innumerable, and the lacking of any of them we may
call evil. Whatever satisfies the reason, the
heart, the imagination, whatever ministers to
health and comfort, whatever offers opportunity
to increase knowledge or power has worth. The
useful, the agreeable, the beautiful, the true are
valuable; but that which is indispensable, with-

out which all else is vain, is moral good, what conscience says ought to be, what we recognize as duty.

Duties are of three kinds: duties of self-respect, of justice, and of benevolence. Self-respect is violated by lying and sensuality; justice by whatever harms the rights of another, whether rights of property or of reputation; benevolence by failure to succor our fellows in their corporal and spiritual needs. To be a man one must rise above merely animal existence, must reverence the reason, the soul which makes him human, and must therefore be truthful, temperate, and chaste; and since humanity can come into being and prosper only in society, he must fulfill the social duties of justice and benevolence. These are principles which all men accept in the inner sanctuary of conscience, and against which only those who are blinded by passion or led astray by a sophistical spirit will attempt to argue. Remove from a city drunkenness and prostitution, theft and dishonesty, lying and deceit, the hardness and inhumanity which greed and sensuality produce, and you have a happy community — one in which peace and order, self-respect and justice, sympathy and loving-kindness prevail; one in which woman and the child are held in honor, in which old age is accompanied by reverence and service, in which the poor and the sick are relieved and consoled. And yet in such a community there would still be evil, there would still be suffering, sorrow, and death.

Why, then, if we could suppress moral evil would the mystery of pain still remain? If a wholly satisfactory explanation of this problem could be given, all the weary weight of this unintelligible world would be lifted from our minds and hearts.

If it is not possible to sweep this black cloud from the heaven of human consciousness, we may at least see rays of light gleam through its rifts. If we look, first of all, into its impenetrable centre where the darkness is most dense, into the realms of moral evil, of sin, we may understand that in a world in which no one could do wrong, no one could do right; that if men are to have freedom of will, — without which they would not be men, — they must have the power to abuse it. What is the highest thing in the world, that which properly constitutes humanity? It is character. Now character cannot be created, it must be formed in the midst of temptation and struggle, in the heat of battle, where, if there is victory, there must also be the possibility of defeat. God may create an innocent being, but not a perfect character. That human goodness may come forth in full power and form there must be free choice, there must be the conflict by which alone moral energy is produced; and if conflict, therefore pain, suffering, and failure. And is not a world in which there is much wickedness and sorrow, but which is also filled with heroic and Godlike men and women, higher than one in which there should be nothing superior to the innocence and ignorance of childish natures?

Of the Captain of our Salvation, the inspired word says: He was made perfect through sufferings. There is indeed no other way that leads to moral excellence. Self-denial, the bearing of the cross, the wearing of the thorny crown, the gibes and mocks of the rabble, the consenting to death rather than to wrong — these are the means whereby character is built, whereby saintliness is made to spring in the soul, whereby the world is redeemed. We are all apprentices, and suffering is our great teacher and master. A man is worth what he has borne. They who have not passed nights of bitter anguish, who have not moistened their bread with tears, know not the heavenly powers. None are wise who have not received the baptism of sorrow. In luxurious climates, where man has nothing to do but to eat and sleep, he is little more than an animal.

What is the universal law of progress but

struggle, effort, labor? And what is this but pain? If there were no obstacles how should there be energy and courage? If Nature presented no difficulties how should man be made intelligent? Pain is danger's signal. It floats above the entrance of the haunts of vice and shame; it waves for the glutton, the drunkard, the adulterer, the tyrant, for criminals of every type. On it is inscribed in letters which none but the blind can fail to read: The wages of sin is death.

Suffering is the mother of wisdom, of pity, of mercy, of the most generous moods and the most tender emotions. They who have never suffered are unfeeling as well as ignorant. The young are cruel because they have not been civilized by sorrow; and they whom sorrow hardens or depraves were ignoble from the start. What joy is there, higher than that of children, which does not derive its fine flavor from the memory of hardships borne and difficulties overcome? We cannot feel that anything is properly ours unless we have made it our own, by industry, patience, perseverance, and foresight, by self-denial and courage. Nothing we inherit rightly belongs to us unless we re-act upon it, suffer for it.

Evil is the foe we have to fight, and by fighting, convert to means of good. By such combat alone is advance made possible. All progress, intellectual, moral, and material, is through conflict with ignorance, passion, and the obstinacy of nature. From less to more, from evil to good. This is the law of human development, individual and social.

But it is in vain that we appeal to philosophy to persuade ourselves that evil is but a means to good, and that all is well. In such a world as this, indeed, good and ill are so intertwined and blended, that we cannot imagine them existing in separateness; but none the less they are distinct and opposite. The ideal which must forever invite us is that of a society in which there shall be no sin nor sorrow nor wrong. To the coming of this kingdom of heaven on earth the noblest look; to bring it nearer the most generous devote all their strength. This is their aim, whether they put their trust in the improvements of institutions or in evolution or in education or in religion. The object is to overcome and suppress whatever is hurtful to man, for we measure all values by human standards; and as we should not think storms, earthquakes, and floods evil, if they wrought no harm to man, so we could not believe God himself to be good if He were not good to man.

Wide and deep as life is life's curse and woe. Millions still believe that those alone are wise who strive to destroy the will to live, and who desire to sink back into the unconscious; that the best is not to be born, or being born, at once to die. But this religion of despair is as foreign to Christian souls as it is to right reason. We know well all life's sadness, all its vanity and misery; but we know also its joy and sweetness, the infinite possibilities it opens to us since the Eternal Father is but the perfect Life.

In our great cities we see the ruin wrought by heartlessness and greed, by drunkenness and prostitution, by corrupt politicians and gamblers, desolation worse than that caused by famine, pest, and war (for the moral evil is blacker and the causes more permanent); yet are we not disheartened but rather incited to new efforts to save bodies and souls from the human devils, whose existence no man or woman can doubt. They are the foes of life, and we are life's lovers and defenders. As they help the animal and the fiend in the breast to kill the man, we appeal to the man to stand forth a living soul, breathed on by God.

The opportunities of laymen for religious work are in some respects greater than those of priests. In the manifold relations they have with one another, in their social intercourse, in their business, means for doing good are given them which are granted more sparingly to the

clergyman. If we trace the history of conver-
sions, we shall find in many instances that they
are due to the silent influence of a layman or of
some gentle and pure-hearted woman. How
often have churches and schools been established
because two or three devoted families have believed and made it possible. One might think it
almost tragical that the masses should be shut
out from the world of high thought and noble
emotion which lies in the great literatures; but
is it not still more tragical that the multitudes
who heard Jesus gladly, who are ahungered and
athirst for God, should be so little acquainted
with the wealth of joy and love and strength
there is in Catholic faith?

This must be so, so long as they remain but
passive members of the Church — of the Church
which needs the hearts and minds and energies
of all its children, whose welfare and progress
depend on the moral condition and spiritual activity, not of the priesthood alone, but of all
Catholics. It is one of the glories of America
that here every man and woman may, if they
will, find fruitful work to do. This is one of
the things that make it the most attractive of
all lands, drawing to itself the millions from all
the earth. In the Catholic Church, too, there is
work for every man and woman; and if opportunity is denied to anyone, it is not because the

Church is not wide and great and rich enough, endowed as she is with the treasures of the mind and heart of Christ, but because those who happen for the time to shape her course and policy, are narrow and unintelligent. A more living participation of all Catholics in the work of the Church is one of our most urgent needs, and whoever might have power to awaken in them a longing for this larger and higher life, and open a way for them in the Church to exercise an influence in the things which concern man's permanent and most essential interests is the leader whom we should all hail with delight and follow with enthusiasm. What brilliant examples of enlightened and beneficent lay action in Catholic affairs we have had in the nineteenth century! It was O'Connell who led the Catholics of Ireland, and I may say of the English-speaking world, out of the bondage of the penal laws. Mallinkrodt and Windthorst were the captains of the hosts that triumphed in the Kultur Kampf. Goerres more than any other man brought about the Catholic revival in Germany nearly a hundred years ago. In France Joseph de Maistre and Chateaubriand reawakened enthusiasm for the Church which seemed to have perished in the general ruin wrought by the Revolution. Brownson is the most vigorous writer who has advocated Catholic principles

in America. In England Dr. Ward, the most
loyal and devoted of believers, surpasses Cardinal Newman in metaphysical insight and in
logical cogency. How nobly Ozanam and Montalembert served the cause of religion! What
these have done, why should not many do, according to the measure of their gifts?

XIII.

AN ORATOR AND LOVER OF JUSTICE.

[Address delivered at the Altgeld Memorial Meeting, April 20, 1902.]

THE disinterested sympathy which we feel for genuine men is a testimony to our own worth, for it proves our faith in character as the paramount good, the solid foundation of man's likeness to God. When we think of the dead whom we have known and loved, we think not of their strength or beauty of body, not of their wealth or position, not of the circum-- stances of their lives, but we think of the self that made them what they were — of their spirit, of the intellectual and moral habits which made them wise, brave, true, loving, and helpful. They may have lived in poverty, in feeble health, in prison; they may have suffered calumny and persecution; they may have died as malefactors; but if in them there was a divine something, an utter devotion to any vital truth or principle, a sacred and disinterested enthusiasm for some good cause, an unwavering and unwearying pursuit of ends which are forever right, their memory is safe. The clouds shall break away and the light which guided them shall shine for thousands; and even their enemies shall learn to admire and be grateful.

In assembling to honor the memory of Governor Altgeld, to profess our faith in his personal worth and in the value of what he has said and done, we honor ourselves, for there is no better proof of noble nature than appreciativeness of noble men.

To be drawn to a genuine man it is not necessary that without reserve we accept his opinions or approve all his actions. All that is required is faith in his intelligence, his honesty, his courage, his good-will, his disinterestedness. It is better to be wrong, inspired by the sense and love of right than to be right, impelled by motives of policy and the worship of vulgar success.

Altgeld doubtless had the qualities which make men interesting and give them influence over their fellows. His aims were high, and the industry and perseverance with which he pursued them were altogether exceptional.

He was eager, all-earnest, untiring, self-forgetful, and devoted. He feared no foe, shrank from no obloquy, turned aside from no danger. Though a politician, he was without policy, never asking himself what might be expedient, but looking only to what he believed to be true, just, and honorable. Though born in Europe, no other public man of his day was so genuinely and so thoroughly American. No question that concerned the general welfare eluded his alert mind. His eye was everywhere, and saw everywhere, through shams and shows into the heart of things. He had a fine scorn of mere wealth, title, and position, and would have taken delight in a beggar who might have had power to make him wiser or better. He abhorred cant, pretense, hypocrisy, and lies. He would not have flattered a king for his crown, nor a plutocrat for all his gold. If a cause was just it commended itself to him all the more because it was unpopular. Like all genuine men, he was modest and without conceit. No honors and no office could rob him of his plain and simple manners. A farmer's boy, a soldier, a lawyer, a politician, a governor, he compelled every situation in which he found himself to minister to the enlargement of his mind and the molding of his character. Deprived of the opportunity of early education, he developed the mental self-activity which is the only means of mental culture, and his intellectual curiosity became at once comprehensive and discriminating. No other politician among us has been so attracted to the things of the mind. Without a knowl-

edge of the classical languages, he was fasci-
nated by the classical literatures. Ability, talent,
genius, character, were what he most admired.
No other public man in our country has written
anything that I should so gladly commend to the
perusal and study of our youth as Altgeld's
" Essay on Oratory," which he published but a
year ago. If we make certain reservations with
regard to the style, it has everything to stamp
it a classical treatise on the subject. In this
brief composition he reveals himself more completely than in anything else he has written.
We have here the passionate lover of eloquence,
one whose thoughts are as urgent as the growth
of wings, who, believing in the healing virtue
of the truth he knows and loves, would communicate it with such directness, force, persuasiveness, and charm, that all shall be compelled
to hearken and become partakers of the divine
gifts. For him oratory is the greatest of the arts
— greater than music, than poetry, than painting, than sculpture. The orator must gather
into unity and harmony all that other artists
achieve separately — must be at once musician,
painter, poet, sculptor, architect; must be able
to take the human mind and heart and imagination for his instrument and play upon it all the
infinite divine cadences of rhythm and reason.
He must stand forth before men as a man clothed

with the resonance of the thunder-crash and with
the searching power of the forked lightning;
must sing to his audience and command them
and subdue them to his every mood and thought;
must have power to transport them into the
midst of sublime scenes, of tumultuous oceans,
of white and eternally serene mountain peaks;
he must know all the melodies that soothe like
the lullabies of mothers; must be able to plead
as only love can plead, — to rouse like a clarion's
note; must be able to find his way through the
labyrinthian windings of the heart of man, with
all its passions and prejudices, and issue forth
heralded as a conqueror. His words must be
as full of music as a poet's, as clear-cut as a
statue, as symmetrical as the noblest monument,
as rightly ordered as an army in battle array;
his thought must unfold itself like the budding
leaves and the blossoming flowers; and from the
centre and heart of it all he must rise and reveal
himself, not as an actor but as a man and mes-
senger sent by God to proclaim truth and vindi-
cate the right. He must have a knowledge of
history, of literature, of religion, of science, of
the world. He must be all alive with the subject he discusses. If his thoughts be not new,
they must glow with a light not seen before;
and they must be pure and high that they may
appeal to what is best in man. He must utter,

not what the arithmetical understanding would suggest, but what the soul would speak to souls. His language must be beautiful; his words simple, chaste, and crystalline; his phrases must sparkle and glow like jewels on the brow of beauty. But he must ever bear in mind that mere vesture can not hide the unreality and vacancy of what is false and vulgar. Right words are born of true thoughts; and true thoughts of noble life. Those alone who take infinite pains can hope to become orators. There is no seeming trifle which may be neglected, for perfection is the result of attention to little things. He who would excel must inure himself to the labor of writing and rewriting what he would utter. The pen is to the mind what the plough is to the field. Ploughs do not sow the seed, but without the culture they give it will not thrive and yield rich harvest, however fertile the soil. When meditation and composition shall have made him familiar with every phase of his subject, lucid order, accurate expression, and copious language will come as the fountains burst and leap in spring. Having aroused and illumined his own spiritual being, he will have a message and the skill rightly to deliver it to his audience; and not to them only, but to the wider world to which the wings of the press shall bear his words.

The public-speaking which has politics and business for its subject is useful and important, but Fame blows not her trumpet above the heads of those who do this work. They are talkers, not orators; fortunate if they talk logically, forcibly, to the point, while they keep themselves free from slang and other offense against the laws of speech. But he who would utter memorable things in perfect form must dwell in higher regions where gleams the light of ideal aims and ends; must think no labor too great, no self-denial too hard, if it help him to become a master. Like the mighty Grecian, he must love solitude, be willing, if need be, to dwell in caves by the resounding shores of the loud ocean; must take for his companions the immortal minds who have left record of themselves in books. He must abstain, train himself like an athlete, and accustom himself to all exercises that invigorate and sharpen the intellect or harden and supple the body. He must stand aloof from the crowds and despise the applause of the vulgar and the notoriety which is within the reach of criminals and prize-fighters. He must be wholly serious and sincere and keep his conscience pure, though he have not bread to eat. Great manhood alone can make great oratory possible. Above all, the orator must be a lover of truth and justice. His

sympathies must go forth to the toilers who do
the world's work and are God's children. Wherever there is oppression and wrong, he must be
ready in the name of the Lord to defend and
make good.

All this springs from the purest spirit of
Altgeld's life. He himself lacked some of the
important qualities which contribute to a public
speaker's success and eminence. His presence
was not commanding; his voice lacked sonor-
ity, modulation, and persuasiveness; his gesticu-
lation was awkward and constrained; his style
was unpolished; his imagination prosaic; his
literary culture defective. He had not the
scholar's fine insight and thorough knowledge
of the best that has been thought and said; and
yet withal he was more truly an orator than
almost any other public man of his day. Eloquence lies not in words and manner, but in the
man himself; and Altgeld was all athrill with
the passion, earnestness, and emotion which
awaken and fix attention while they create interest. It was not merely the things he believed in,
admired, and loved, but rather the thoroughness
and intensity of his convictions, that lifted him
to higher planes of thought and feeling, and
gave to his utterances a significance and charm
which are beyond the reach of rhetoricians and
demagogues. With all his heart he loved truth

and hated lies; loved justice and hated iniquity.
As he was capable of giving his life for what
he held to be right, so had he infinite power of
scorn for tricksters and spoilsmen, for palterers
and beggars of the approval of men. He knew
the blessedness of being hated and calumniated
for fidelity to conscience. The best men are
made great by the obstacles they surmount, by
the enemies they withstand. Nearly all our
speakers tread the paths of dalliance, hold their
ears to the ground to catch the murmur of the
crowd, make brave shots at safe objects, apolo-
gize if by chance they utter the naked truth;
but here was one for whom right and wrong
are parted by eternal laws, for whom compro-
mise is treason, and connivance apostasy from
God and the soul. Pallid, feeble in body, over-
worked, and overwrought by the intensity of his
own nature and too eager mind, he faced corruption and a hostile opinion begotten of the spirit
of Mammonites and time-servers with the heroic
courage of confessors and martyrs. He knew
better than anyone that throughout America
and Europe his name was associated with doctrines and practices which he abhorred, that he
was a safe mark for the conscienceless fling of
every hireling of the press, that to be his friend
was to incur suspicion of not being respectable,
but he faltered not; and though fallen on evil

days and slandered by evil tongues, though over-
taken by poverty and sneered at by the idolators
of success, he continued to confront with dauntless courage all the fosterers of lies and corruption, all the contrivers of oppression and wrong,
all the apologists of conquest and inhumanity.
He had a heart as tender as a woman's; a soul
as dauntless as a hero's. Whatever concerned
the poor, the weak, the disinherited, had his
earnest attention and sympathies. His faith
in the people was profound, and he believed that
democratic government may be so organized and
administered as to make it a blessing to all, and
first of all to those who most need protection
and fair opportunity because they are the most
defenseless and the most easily wronged. He
studied the question of education, and thoroughly
understood that liberty of teaching is the foundation on which all our other liberties rest. He
did not, I think, sufficiently understand — nor
has any other American statesman sufficiently
understood — that if education does not form
character and promote conduct, it fails in the
most vital point. Intelligence is not enough; it
is not the most indispensable thing in human
life, individual or social; but when one considers
the infinite misery and ruin which have been
wrought and which continue to be wrought by
ignorance and stupidity, he is persuaded that

it is not possible to have too much zeal for
the diffusion of knowledge and the spread of
enlightenment. No other governor of Illinois
has devoted so much serious thought or so much
good-will to the management and improvement
of our penal and reformatory institutions, and
the great good he has done in this matter can
hardly be other than permanent. How jealous
he was of our constitutional rights and liberties!
How quick to resent even the appearance of
infringement upon them!

He knew and felt intensely that the good
which we cherish for ourselves we should not
take from others; and hence he abhorred all
wars of conquest, however specious the pretexts
with which the real motives are cloaked. He
applauded the expulsion of the Spaniard from
Cuba that the inhabitants of the island might
have opportunity to establish a government of
their own; and he held that justice and honor
and every genuine American impulse demand
that the same right should be conceded to the
Filipinos. What ineffable disgust, what right-
eous wrath the crimes of some of our officers
and soldiers (which have affixed a brand of infamy on the name of America) would have
aroused within him!

It was altogether fitting that he should die
while pleading for the Boers — the most heroic

patriots and the victims of the greatest crime against liberty and justice, against humanity itself, which has been committed within the memory of living men; a crime which Americans more than any other people would have denounced to the whole world with clamorous indignation and abhorrence, had not conscience made cowards of us all.

Here, then, let me close, while I salute, with admiration, respect, and reverence the memory of a genuine and heroic man — the truest servant of the people and the most disinterested politician whom Illinois has known since Lincoln died.

XIV.

ST. BEDE.

[Delivered at the dedication of St. Bede College,
Peru, Ill.]

THE founding of St. Bede's College by the
order of St. Benedict in the Valley of the
Illinois is not merely an interesting event, it is
also a fact which is pregnant with promise of
good.

From this spot we have a view of a country
which is as fair as it is fertile, and which,
already populous, is destined to become the busi-
est hive of human industry. Beneath the black
soil lie inexhaustible coal-measures hardly
blacker. The climate is at once wholesome and
invigorating, and the people who have taken
possession of this favored region have in their
veins the blood which for more than a thousand
years has nourished the hearts of conquerors
and subduers. They belong to that race which
has never quailed before hostile man or forbid-
ding nature, and which has acknowledged as
its superior only the almighty God. The State

of Illinois, which half a century ago was almost a wilderness, is now cultivated like Belgium or Lombardy. Its villages are counted by the thousand, its towns by the hundred; and whithersoever we turn we behold streaming in the air the black pennon of the mighty engine which bears over the trembling plain bounteous gifts to pour them into the lap of peoples which are separated from us by oceans and by every divergence of tongue and character. We are in the heart of the great continent, in the centre of commerce and manufacture, with lines of communication, east and west, north and south. There are interests too, of a more spiritual nature, which cluster here to dedicate this spot to religion and to the cause of education. Along this valley passed the early explorers and discoverers, who seemed already to foresee that the rivers which make an open highway between the lakes and the gulf, were destined by Providence to help to bring about a union of hearts and minds among millions of men, who should have but one law as they adore but one God. In the plain which lies beneath us the holy Sacrifice was offered and the gospel was preached when the colonists of New England were still engaged in fierce conflicts with the Indians, when feuds and revolts were threatening the existence of the struggling settlements of Virginia and

Maryland, when Manhattan Island (which the Dutch had bought from the natives for twenty-four dollars) did not contain a population of fifteen hundred souls. From the College windows "Starved Rock" looms before us, overlooking the valley where stood the original Kaskaskia when Father Marquette, the discoverer of the Mississippi, established the mission of the Immaculate Conception, and on Holy Thursday, in the year 1675, in the presence of two thousand warriors and countless women and children, said the first Mass ever celebrated in Illinois. This, alas, was the last act of his noble and heroic life, for almost immediately afterwards he set forth on his journey northward only to be taken from his birchen canoe to die in the wilderness.

He was followed by Father Allouez, the founder of many missions, who, on the third of May, 1676, erected in the midst of the village a cross twenty-five feet high, which stood for years in the plain that stretches away from the little town of Utica. Here, too, Father Ribourde, a noble Burgundian and the companion of La Salle, preached the gospel, and fell beneath the tomahawk, when the Illinois fled before the terrible Iroquois. Here also labored Father Rale, who more than a quarter of a century later was murdered by the English, while offering his life as a sacrifice for his beloved Abenakis. Associations of yet another kind which are more intimately related to the history of our own country, also gather here; for the spot on which we stand was once the property of our greatest orator, — of him whose lofty thought and majestic style have clothed the constitutional principles of our government with the splendor of genius, — Daniel Webster, our least mortal mind, who in his high prescience foresaw the diruption of our country, and saw that God would make it whole again.

Those who have chosen this spot as the site of a college and monastery have not acted without wisdom. The sons of St. Benedict inherit a taste for the beauties of nature. Their cradle on Monte Cassino overlooks the dreaming hills and the rich valleys which stretch far away to dip themselves in the blue waters of the Bay of Naples; and from that eminence, where they supplanted Apollo, the god of light and beauty, they have taken flight and, like the honey-laden ever-busy bees, have settled upon a thousand heights, and on a thousand plains, to make them vocal with the ceaseless song of praise and the most pleasant noise of labor. The very ruins of the places where they abode make beautiful and consecrate the regions which lie about them. The highest symbol and embodiment of

man's spiritual and infinite nature, of his faith
in God and moral consciousness, is the Church;
but the mightiest and most heavenly leader of
the champions of the soul, of the followers of
the Blessed Christ, is Saint Benedict. If we
look to what he has accomplished he stands forth
from the ranks of the saints, as Cæsar stands
forth from the ranks of the heroes. As the
great Roman shaped the course of Empire for
more than a thousand years, so the founder of
Western monasticism directed for centuries the
progress and development of Christian life and
civilization. More than all others he understood
how to harmonize man's yearning for temporal
power and dominion, for knowledge and freedom, with the genius of the religion of Christ,
whose eye is forever bent on the eternal and
infinite. The history of his order is the highest
evidence that faith and love, humility and patience, are the saving principles. They fertilize
the earth, illumine the mind, strengthen the
heart, and people heaven with elect souls. From
his brotherhood sprang the two popes who in
their influence upon the Church take precedence
of all others — Gregory the Great and Gregory
VII. St. Maur, a disciple of St. Benedict,
carried the order to France, where in a short
time it absorbed the flourishing communities
founded by St. Columbanus, and spread rapidly

throughout the Frankish kingdoms. St. Augustin carried it to England, and it became the paramount influence in converting and molding the Anglo-Saxon race. St. Wilfrid, St. Willibrord and St. Boniface carried it to Holland and Germany, and these great Benedictines hold their undisputed place in history as the apostles of the Teutonic peoples. From the tomb of Boniface at Fulda, the monastic brotherhood spread through the whole Fatherland, as in England it spread from Canterbury; and wherever the monks encamped, the forest was felled, the marsh was drained, the school was built, and the barbarous populations were brought under the influence of religion and law.

In the midst of universal ignorance these monasteries became the centres of learning, the storehouses of all that remained of sacred and profane literature; and from them there issued forth a ceaseless stream of enlightened teachers and wise rulers. The knowledge of what was then accomplished led Charlemagne to decree that a school should be attached to every monastery and every cathedral throughout the empire. In this apostolic epoch, in the history of the order, the Benedictines were the heroes who, amidst the irruptions of lawless hordes, amid the clash of arms and the wild confusion of unrestrained cruelty and lust, stood undaunted,

their hearts raised to heaven, while their hands
held the plough and the pen. They were the
men of light and reason, who looking up to the
Father in heaven, put their trust in knowledge
and labor: they appealed from the brutal courage of the barbarian, who exulted amid the ruins
he had made, to the all-conquering moral power
of religious faith, which makes man patient and
strong in the consciousness that he works with
God to upbuild an enduring society, where those
who know and love dwell with the Eternal.
These monastic schools taught the whole cycle
of human knowledge: philosophy, theology,
mathematics, natural science, poetry, rhetoric,
and music, as well as classical and sacred literature. Of Alcuin, one of these monks, the
friend and counsellor of Charlemagne, Guizot
says: "He is a monk, a deacon, the light of
the contemporaneous church; but he is at the
same time a scholar, a classical man of letters."
When we reflect that the Benedictines, in their
heroic age, to perfect faith, to blamelessness of
life, to dauntless courage, to the spirit of tireless
labor, joïned the best culture of mind then possible, we need not stop to examine into the
causes of their phenomenal success. In spite
of the jealousy and envy which great merit ex-
cites, true worth wins its way to the heart of
man. We fatally turn to those who have the

power and the will to help us; for we all are
weak, and would be strong; we all are ignorant,
and would have knowledge; we all are timid
and confused, and would follow those who have
an eye to see and a heart to lead. When men
are pure, devout, and humble, and also enlightened, intrepid, and active, the world will hearken
to their voice and drink the inspiration of their
lives; and those who, by habitual self-denial
attain to knowledge and virtue, become the natural guides and rulers of their fellows. In what
marvelous degree the order of St. Benedict has
succeeded in giving such men to the world we
may see at a glance. By the middle of the four-
teenth century, twenty-four of its members had
sat upon the Chair of St. Peter, two hundred had
been cardinals, seven thousand had been archbishops, fifteen thousand had been bishops, and
upon more than fifty thousand the title of saint
had been conferred by the voice of the people
or the Church. To them chiefly the world is
indebted for the conversion of the Germanic
peoples, for the upbuilding of the kingdoms of
France and England; to them for bringing under
cultivation vast tracts of waste land, for training
innumerable barbarous populations to till the
soil; to them for keeping alive in the West the
traditions of intellectual culture and for preserving the classical writings. Every monas-

tery, according to the rule of St. Benedict, was
to have a library, and every monk to possess a
pen and tablet. To them also the world is indebted for their fearless insistence upon the
principle that neither obscure birth, nor poverty,
nor bodily weakness is a barrier to eminence;
that opportunity should be given to slaves and
beggars, who, if they are found worthiest,
should be made popes and kings. To them,
notably to Gregory the Great, Guido D'Arrezzo,
and Ockenheim, we are indebted for the cultivation and improvement of sacred music, of which
our modern music, the disinctive art of the
nineteenth century, is but a development. I will
not, however, insist upon the services which the
Benedictines have rendered, nor shall I attempt
to conceal the abuses, which, here and there, and
again and again, have crept into the order during the fourteen centuries of its existence.

A religious order is but a human institution,
and the Church itself, which is of divine origin,
has its epochs of weakness and decadence. I do
not now recall the name of the cardinal, who,
when there was question of giving the highest
ecclesiastical sanction to the society of Jesus,
opposed it on the ground that the good done
by religious orders in the fervor of their early
years is more than counterbalanced by the harm
they do when, as it always happens, discipline

becomes relaxed and the heroic virtue of the founders and first disciples gives place to indifference and self-indulgence. Whatever truth there may be in this view, it did not meet with the approval of the Pope, although a committee of cardinals, of whom Reginald Pole was one, had but two years before made a report to him, in which they declared that they were of opinion that all the religious orders should be suppressed.

It was a disciple of St. Benedict, himself a saint, and a monk and a pope as well, Gregory the Great, who wrote: " It is better to have scandal than a lie "; and the monks who wrote the annals of their orders did not seek to conceal the abuses which had crept into them. " I contend," says St. Bernard, " not against, but for the monastic order, when I expose the vices of men who make part of it." It was left to the half-doubting faith of weaker ages to imagine that the best way to make wrong right is to deny its existence.

It is but truth, however, to say that the abuses which have enfeebled and tainted the life of so many orders, have been misunderstood and exaggerated. They have nearly always arisen from the invasion of the temporal power. Kings and princes and statesmen, under the vicious system known as the *Commende,* which began to prevail early in the middle ages and spread widely throughout Europe, claimed the right to place their favorites as superiors over religious houses, and under the rule of such men the vices of the world fatally made their way into the sanctuaries of religion. But when the worst is said even of those whom the world thus corrupted, all that can be truthfully affirmed is that they became self-indulgent and indolent, following the bent of human nature, which inclines to the love of ease and of the good things of earth, drifting down to a sluggish life of mere sensation and thought-lessness. "Vain will be any endeavor," says Montalembert, the historian of "The Monks of the West," "to alter the distinctive character of their social historical part, which is that of having lived to do good. Humanly speaking, they have done nothing else: all their career is occupied with peopling deserts, protecting the poor, and enriching the world. Sadly degenerated towards their decline, much less active and less industrious than in their origin, they never became less charitable. Where is the country, where is the man whom they have injured? where are the monuments of their oppression? the memorials of their rapacity? If we follow the furrow which they have dug through history, we shall find everywhere but the traces of their beneficence." But to have

done is of small account. Ingratitude to individuals is but a form of that universal un-
thankfulness which makes us look with a pity
akin to contempt upon whatever thing or institution which, having been great and strong, is
now reduced to nullity. Men will not love the
Church or its religious orders for what may
have been done by them. The old, who are
sinking beneath life's rapid current, may seek
to prolong a feeble existence by cherishing memories of things that have passed away, but the
young and vigorous turn with eager expectancy
to what is now capable of nourishing the mind,
the heart, and the soul. Our religion is divine,
not because it has blossomed forth in former
ages, in the lives of virgins and apostles, of
martyrs and confessors; nor yet because through
its inspiration, genius in every form of artistic
expression has clothed the highest thought with
perfect beauty — breathing harmony, giving
movement to stone, speech to canvas, and to
human language the power to utter immortal
truth and Godlike love, in cadence and melody,
which like the music of higher worlds, like the
cradle-songs of childhood's lost paradise, linger
forever in memory to soothe, uplift, and console
the heart of man; but it is divine because it
contains the germs of an everpresent, infinite
life, which seems to wane and die only to be

born again, amid other environments, with a
vigor and a beauty which are always fresh and
delightful.

And it is the glory of the order of St. Benedict
that though like the Church, it has again and
again seemed about to be overwhelmed by the
calamities of the times and the force of human
passion, yet like the fair mother of souls, it has
again and again in the long course of ages, risen
superior to fate, and gathering into its ranks
the children of new generations, addressed itself
to deeds of light and beneficence.

When nearly three centuries after its foundation, the troubled and barbarous state of the
world had led to a relaxation of discipline
in innumerable monasteries, St. Benedict of
Amian arose and finally succeeded in reforming
almost the entire order, which then entered
upon its most brilliant period of service to the
cause of religion and civilization, of science and
literature.

When the Empire of the Franks was invaded
by the Normans and the Huns, from the West
and the East, who pillaged the convents and
dispersed the monks, the general ruin brought
disorder also in the cloisters. The ninth and
tenth centuries are the age of darkness and confusion. But even in this epoch of chaos a new
and salutary movement was begun among the

Benedictines.   Hitherto each monastery had stood alone and independent; but now mother-houses were constituted, which imposed their rule upon the affiliated convents and watched over the observance of discipline.   Upon this plan the congregation of Cluny was established in France, the congregation of Camaldoli in Italy, the congregation of Vallombrosa in Tuscany, and the congregation of Hirschau in Germany, which have all a great and noble history.

In England a similar reformation was brought about by St. Dunstan, who caused the old life in its peace and fruitfulness to flourish again.   During the eleventh century new branches spráng from the parent trunk such as those of Granmont and Citeaux, the latter of which the genius and courage of St. Bernard pushed so vigorously forward that it rapidly spread through Europe, and within a century of its foundation embraced eight hundred rich abbeys; and when towards the end of the twelfth century its immense wealth began to act unfavorably upon discipline, John de la Barrière, after a considerable lapse of time, succeeded in effecting a reform which gave rise to the Feuillants in France and to the Bernardines in Italy.   Another salutary reformation brought about by Didier de la Cour in the Convent of St. Vanne, in the sixteenth century, renewed

the religious life of the Benedictine monasteries
of Lorraine, Alsace, and Burgundy. Intimately
associated with St. Vanne is the reformation
introduced into the convent of St. Augustin of
Limoges in the early part of the seventeenth
century, giving rise to the celebrated congregation of St. Maur, which embraced a hundred and twenty-four abbeys, the centres of a
literary activity that extended to every branch
of science, and enriched the world with works
which will remain as monuments of patient
research and profound erudition.

The French Revolution, upheaving and over-
turning everything, suppressed the Benedictine
order in France, Spain, and Germany; as in
England the Protestant Reformation had swept
away its hundred and eighty-six abbeys and
priories. But this order has again sprung to
life and established itself in the chief countries
of Europe. It was introduced into Pennsyl-
vania in 1846 by a colony of monks from Ba-
varia; and from the Abbey of St. Vincent it
has spread through the country in many direc-
tions; and that its activity has not ceased the
opening of this College of St. Bede to-day is
evidence enough.

Here, indeed, there is little to recall the conditions, physical, moral, and intellectual, which
existed when the Benedictine monasteries and

schools were established throughout Europe in
the early middle ages. No barbarous hordes
will come to destroy these buildings; kings and
princes will not have power to appoint here unworthy superiors, and the people by whom they
are surrounded are neither ignorant nor pagan;
for the marvelous material development of the
West has not been unaccompanied by religious
and intellectual improvement. If the thousands
of Indians who heard the first Mass said in
Illinois have with their descendants passed away
to sink into the ocean of oblivion and nothing-
ness, the faith has not perished with them. On
the contrary it lives in this great State with an
energy and freshness which might make us forget that it comes down to us from ages when
our rude ancestors had not yet emerged from
their dense forests to overrun the world and to
fill it with terror and ruin. There are in Illinois
to-day more than six hundred Catholic churches
and nearly seven hundred priests, and our
schools, asylums and institutions of beneficence
are scattered all over the State. And to perceive
how rapid is the development of our ecclesiastical organization, we need but consider that in
this diocese of Peoria, where at the time of its
formation, fourteen years ago, there were not
fifty priests, including those who were in the
five counties since added to it, there are now a

hundred and thirty, and that whereas then there
were not in its present territory more than ninety
churches, there are now a hundred and seventy;
and it is but truth to say that among the strong
and active people in the midst of whom we live,
none are more intrepid, more laborious, more
eager to take advantage of whatever opportunities are offered to promote the spiritual and
temporal welfare of their fellow-men than the
Catholic priests. They instruct, they guide,
they build, and while they insist upon righteousness and plead for interests which are eternal,
nothing that concerns the welfare of man is
foreign to their thought. I will not speak of
their patriotism, for to boast of one's patriotism
is to lay one's self open to suspicion, and is
besides as much a breach of good taste as to
boast of one's virtue; but I think I may say
without risk that they believe in freedom and in
education as they believe in God and in Christ.

In their name and with them, Right Reverend
and Reverend Fathers, I welcome you to this diocese of Peoria. You come, in a sense, to be our
teachers and guides; for whatever fervor of
faith and piety, whatever illumination of mind
is shed from here, will warm and light us all.

The principles which underlie the religious
life are divine. It is forever and everywhere
right to be gentle and lowly of heart, to be obe-

dient to law, to be chaste in thought and act, to prefer the good which lies within us to whatever is merely external. To pray, to toil, to study, to write, to speak, to live plainly and to think nobly, because such life is Godlike and because it brings blessings to men — this is your aim, this your vocation: to spread peace and faith, freedom and good-will, science and art, light and life — this is your work.

"Your rule," says the most eloquent voice ever uplifted in advocacy of religious truth, " is an epitome of Christianity, a learned·and mysterious abridgment of all the doctrines of the gospel, all the institutions of the holy fathers, and all the counsels of perfection. Here prudence and simplicity, humility and courage, severity and gentleness, freedom and dependence eminently appear. Here correction has all its firmness, condescension all its charm, command all its vigor, and obedience all its repose; silence its gravity, words their grace, strength its exercise, and weakness its support; and yet always, my fathers, he calls it a beginning to keep you always in holy fear." You bring to our young and vigorous life, the charm and mystery of the past, the poetry, and romance of the marvelous creative middle age. You knew the Rome of the Cæsars before it had been despoiled by the invader and the envious tooth of all-destroying time. You were present when century after century the onrushing hordes trampled whatever was great or beautiful beneath the hoofs of their wild steeds. You saw the new order begin to take form, as islet after islet emerged from the chaotic waste, and hearkening to the voice of religion, men dared again to hope. You saw the splendid pageantry of that wondrous world which lives again in the pages of Froissart and Shakspere, of Bocaccio and Dante. Emperors and kings, queens and princesses, have taken the habit of your order and become your brothers and sisters. You have spoken truth to popes and defied tyrants. Of all the heroes whom Carlyle has praised, none I think, was so near to his heart, as Abbot Samson, that typical Benedictine, whose foot was planted on the solid earth to maintain all justice and to defend all right, and whose faith in the unseen world was as sure and serene as though he had gazed upon it with bodily eye. You are of ancient and noble lineage; the awful weight of a glorious past rests upon you; adown the centuries a cloud of virgins and apostles, of martyrs and heroes, whisper in the silent regions of the soul, bidding you gird yourselves for the ceaseless struggle for moral freedom from enslaving passion, for mental illumination that will dispel all-confounding ignorance. The one great purpose of all institutions of learning is to bring young and sensitive natures into living, daily and hourly contact with generous and enlightened minds. This is the vital part of education, and all else is mere machinery. Ah! may the eager yearning youths who shall crowd these halls find here as friends and teachers, men, the bare thought of whom shall have power, like fame, to raise the clear spirit "to scorn delights and live laborious days."

But to exhort is to reproach, and I gladly turn to the sweet and placid countenance of our Venerable Bede, as he is brought before me by the most meditative and thoughtful of poets:

> " But what if one, through grove or flowery mead,
> Indulging thus at will the creeping feet
> Of a voluptuous indolence, should meet
> Thy hovering shade, O Venerable Bede!
> The saint, the scholar, from a circle freed
> Of toil stupendous, in a hallowed seat
> Of learning, where thou heard'st the billows beat
> On a wild coast, rough monitors to feed
> Perpetual industry.   Sublime Recluse
> The recreant soul that dares to shun the debt
> Imposed on human kind, must first forget
> Thy diligence, thy unrelaxing use
> Of a long life, and in the hour of death
> The last dear service of thy passing breath."

Bede is the fairest and noblest figure of the age to which he belongs.   Born in an obscure corner of the world, of the Anglo-Saxon race, which half a century before was still hidden in the darkness of ignorance and idolatry, he stands forth not only as a historical writer of the first rank, the sole source of our knowledge of a people whose deeds have changed the earth and filled it with their fame; but he is also a scholar of wide culture, intimately acquainted with whatever in his day was best worth knowing. A theologian, an exegete, a historian, writing and speaking at pleasure in prose or verse, in Anglo-Saxon or in Latin, he knew besides whatever it was then possible to know of philosophy and science. Quotations from Plato, Cicero, Seneca, from Virgil, Ovid, Lucretius fall from his pen as readily as the words of the gospel itself. He is, in truth, as Edmund Burke entitles him, the " Father of English learning," the typical scholar such as the English universities have always sought to produce. In the midst of a life of ceaseless intellectual toil he still preserves the fresh fervor of his youthful piety, closing the list of his literary labors with this touching prayer: " Oh, good Jesus, who hast deigned to refresh my soul with the sweet streams of knowledge, grant that I may one day mount to Thee, who art the source of all wisdom, to remain forever in thy divine presence." And what simple winsomeness there is in these words concerning himself: "Having been sent by my family at the age of seven years, to be educated, I have ever since lived in this monastery, where I have diligently pondered the Scriptures; and while observing the rule and chanting daily in choir, I have always felt it to be a pleasant thing either to learn, or to teach or to write." His death was as beautiful as his life was fair and fruitful. During all his illness he ceased not from teaching and dictating, and when the evening of the last day was come, one of his disciples said to him: "Beloved master, there remains but one word to write." "Write it quickly," he answered; and when it was completed the disciple said: "Now it is finished." "You say truly, it is finished," the Saint replied. "Take my head in your arms and turn me, for I have great consolation in looking toward the holy place where I have prayed so much." Then he passed to the unseen world.

Oh, happy omen, that this college and monastery are to bear a name so full of warmth and light! Here too shall be found servants of God, lovers of men, bright stars of the monastic brotherhood, who, here where the echo of the war whoop died away but yesterday, shall walk in the ways of peace and of wisdom, shall teach knowledge and shed upon fair young souls the light of faith and the glow of heavenly love.

As the harvest reaped in these fertile fields is sent over seas and oceans to nourish millions; as the coal underlying our feet is distributed through distant regions of the North, to warm and cheer the homes of thousands, so shall there gather here from year to year a swarm of youths athirst, who, drinking deep at this open fountain of truth and spiritual life, shall scatter through the land — centres of influence from which high thought, true courage, and noble aims shall radiate. If I, who by birth, by training, and by love, not less than by the visible environments of my actual home, belong to the West, may be permitted to express an opinion upon the character of the western people, I will say that those persons mistake who imagine that the energy which has wrought the material transformation of which the wide world is witness, is that of a people which can ever rest content with merely material achievements. Whether our origin be Anglo-Saxon, Celtic, or German, we come of the world's best blood, belong to races to whom the ideals of religion and culture, of freedom and righteousness have ever appealed with irresistible force.

If, with incredible industry we have, within half a century, leveled the mountains and filled the valleys and made straight the ways, who can doubt that all this has been done to enable

a free people, unhindered and unhampered, to
enter upon the infinitely more arduous task of
rising to heights of intellectual and moral excellence? The spirit of democracy bids us look
at the man, not at his birth or surroundings:
but if — while we think lightly of aristocratic
descent, of the trappings of office, the vain sound
of titles, and the vulgar show of wealth — the
best culture of mind and the noblest devotion of
soul leave us unsympathetic and unmoved, what
power can save us from becoming hopelessly
common and inferior? Ah! we shall not rest
content until religion infuse through all our life
the charm of reverence and gentleness, of
modest and polite breeding, making impossible
the coarseness and vulgarity which are still so
manifest; until the best culture, opening to our
view the whole past of the race and all the
realms of nature, break down the hard and narrow walls which confine every ignorant soul,
giving to each one of us the dignity, greater than
that of princes, which belongs to virtue and
wisdom. The impetus given to our material
development is so irresistible that we cannot
imagine its progress should be arrested; and the
machinery of our political life will be kept in
some kind of order, we cannot doubt, by the
patriots who are ever willing to sacrifice their
ease for the care and worry of office; but what

we need above all things, and what I believe we most yearn for, is the man, the influence, the institution, with power to nourish the life of the soul; to give us faith, hope, and love; to give us wide knowledge and great thoughts; to strengthen and refine our sense of beauty; to make us appreciative of whatever is true or divine or fair or noble.

For some such purpose, this college has been founded. May God's blessing rest upon it; may good men's hands be outstretched to help it; may those who year after year shall enter its halls return to their homes, like merchants from distant lands, laden with rich store of wisdom and love; and some day, when we who are here shall sleep with our fathers in the cool earth, let a loving hand write above its portals Bede's epitaph:

> " O Bede, God's servant and bright star
> Of the monastic brotherhood !
> From regions which do lie afar,
> To the whole Church thou hast brought good."

15